Tivoli Bays
Dutchess County, NY

Boundary of Hudson River National
Estuarine Research Reserve as shown in 1993 Final
Management Plan of NYSDEC/NOAH

Map adapted from U.S. Geological Survey Map,
Saugerties, N.Y., 1963.

CHANGING TIDES

TIVOLI BAYS: A Hudson River Wetland

Text and Photographs by ESTHER KIVIAT

Foreword by John Winthrop Aldrich

PURPLE MOUNTAIN PRESS   Fleischmanns, New York

CHANGING TIDES: Tivoli Bays, A Hudson River Wetland

FIRST EDITION
1999

Published by
Purple Mountain Press, Ltd.
Main Street, Post Office Box E3
Fleischmanns, New York 12430-0378
914-254-4062
914-254-4476 (fax)
E-mail: Purple@catskill.net
http://www.catskill.net/purple

Library of Congress Cataloging-in-Publication Data

Kiviat, Esther.
    Changing tiedes : Tivoli Bays : a Hudson River wetland / text and
photographs by Esther Kiviat ; forword by John Winthrop Aldrich. --
1st ed.
        p.   cm.
    Includes bibliographical references (p.   ).
    1. Natural history--New York (State)--Tivoli Bays.   I. Title.
    ISBN 0-916346-67-6 (pbk.)
QH105.N5K58   1999
508.747'33--dc21   99-10524
                                                CIP

Book Design by Esther Kiviat and Lucille C. Nickerson

Publication Assistant: Nicholas C. Westlund

Manufactured in the United States of America.
Printed on acid-free paper.
2 4 5 3 1

Cover photograph: *Marsh and Mountains, South Pool, Tivoli North Bay*
Frontispiece photograph: *Spatterdock and Clouds, Late Afternoon, Tivoli North Bay*
Photograph facing contents page: *Dried Winter Grass, Edge of Tivoli North Bay*

The opinions expressed in *Changing Tides*
are those of the author and do not neces-
sarily represent the views of the sponsors.

FOR MY HUSBAND CHARLES
1903 - 1995

Born in Stapleton, Staten Island, at the very edge of New York Harbor, Charlie grew up with a life-long love for the sea, the harbor, and the estuarine Hudson River, where the oceanic tides flow unceasingly in and out.

CONTENTS

FOREWORD

One day in 1952, when I was about ten years old, my father bundled me into the car and drove lickety-split from our farm at Barrytown to Cruger Island Road, in the hope of showing me something he had seen there a short while before. What it was he wouldn't say, but his excitement and anticipation quickly became my own. He had been out that way early in the morning–perhaps shotgunning for ducks from his little sculling boat on the Tivoli South Bay, with his decoys deployed and his duck call squawking.

He parked midway down the road and we started walking. Then we saw it! A few hundred yards to the north, alighting on an upper limb of a tree and soon taking flight again–an eagle! It was probably a juvenile American bald, my first sighting outside a zoo, an experience I would not have again for thirty years. That day Cruger Island became a special place for me.

Not long after, a relative paid a visit. Dr. Conrad Chapman of Boston had grown up at Barrytown and was familiar with Cruger Island and the Tivoli Bays. He told us about a fledgling national organization of which he was a founding board member. The purpose of the Nature Conservancy was to identify and preserve through private action habitats of biological importance, and he was scouting for candidates.

High on his agenda for this pioneering enterprise was Cruger Island and its flanking bays, but nothing was to come of his efforts there.

The area has long been of high repute among bird-watchers, botanists, and those interested in natural history and archeology. In the summer of 1868, the parents of nine-year-old Theodore Roosevelt rented a house overlooking the Tivoli South Bay. In a boyhood journal which T.R. started at that time, he recorded his observations and specimen collecting on solitary field trips to Cruger Island and along the shore of the bay. Decades later Franklin Roosevelt would go birding on Cruger Island with Rhinebeck ornithologist Maunsell Crosby and others.

In the mid-1970s I had the privilege of accompanying Stanley J. Smith, distinguished long-time Curator of Botany at the New York State Museum, on a field trip in quest of *Micranthemum micranthemoides*, a tiny wetland plant previously found only once in New York State–in Tivoli North Bay–a generation earlier. If it survived and could be located, Mr. Smith believed it would be the rarest species of native flora in New York. In this we did not succeed. To date the plant has not been rediscovered anywhere in the state, but many other interesting plants were noted by this preeminent field botanist, who was also a passionate believer in the conservation of habitat and natural diversity and the use of nature preserves in environmental education.

The eagle, Dr. Chapman, Mr. Smith, and the elusive *Micranthemum* were all likely in the back of my mind when I started to press for pubic acquisition of the area in my capacity as Executive Secretary of New York State's Nature and Historical Preserve Trust, which operated from my aerie in the Office of the Commissioner of Environmental Conservation. Central Hudson Gas and Electric Corporation had acquired the property some years previously as an intended site for a nuclear power plant, but had come to understand that ecological considerations would prevent such a use of the land. Central Hudson was persuaded to sell, the Trust's Board approved the use of bond funds for the acquisition, federal grant assistance was obtained, and in 1981 the Tivoli Bays State Nature Preserve came into the public domain. Since 1982 it has been managed as part of the Hudson River National Estuarine Research Reserve. Mr. Smith, Dr. Chapman, the two Roosevelts, and the eagle would each find this gratifying.

There is, as well, a cultural history of importance associated with this neighborhood, most notably ten thousand years of Native American occupation and its record left behind in the ground. Dutch navigators identify promontories and peninsulas as "hoeks," and it is believed that Red Hook takes its name from a charting of Cruger Island one September in the seventeenth century when the sumac and Virginia creeper were ablaze. About 1764, Captain Abram Van Benthuysen owned most of the land now comprising the Research Reserve, Montgomery Place, and Bard College, and built a substantial house on the south side of lower Cruger Island Road that was referred to as "Van Benthuysen's Castle." The island and its environs are significant contributing elements in the state's Mid-Hudson Shorelands Scenic District (1981) and in the Hudson River National Historic Landmark District (1990), the establishment of each having been a process in which I was lucky to play a part.

While sailing with my father in his beloved old sloop in the 1950s, we would occasionally anchor off the southern end of Cruger Island, and the family would row ashore to explore the "false Mayan ruins" or the jumbled remains of the Cruger house. Sailing in his iceboats on the frozen river also brought us into view of the island, as it does still—only nowadays ice conditions seem to confine us to the South Bay. My father relished telling anecdotes about the Crugers, some of which came to him in his youth from a Cruger cousin who lived in Barrytown, Euphemia Van Rensselaer Wyatt. Mrs. Wyatt (one of whose daughters is the actress Jane Wyatt) recorded these family recollections in an unpublished memoir toward the end of her life.

Having related my involvements with Cruger Island and the Tivoli Bays over the years, it only remains to say that what we have always lacked is a readable, concise introduction to this special place, to its diverse natural communities, its cycles of life and its seasonal dress, the dynamic of the estuary, and the traces and stories of man's intervention today, yesterday, and in time immemorial. With this book, Esther Kiviat has wonderfully filled the need. Her lyrical, lucid writing, no less than her precise, vivid photography—both taking the reader through a twelve-month on the island and its adjacent lands and waters—will prove an irresistible lure in getting us out of our armchairs and onto our island. Make no mistake about it: the island and the bays *are* ours, and the better we understand and appreciate this treasure, the better care we will take of it; the better care we take of it, the better it will nourish our spirit and the well-being of those who follow us. Let Esther Kiviat be our guide.

John Winthrop Aldrich
New York State Deputy Commissioner of Historic Preservation
Town of Red Hook Historian

Among many myths about storied Cruger Island is that Henry Hudson anchored off the tip of the island to trade with the natives on his voyage of discovery up the river in 1609. A replica of Hudson's ship, the Half Moon, is shown at right. It recently visited the Kingston Maritime Center, across the river from Tivoli Bays.

Gene Heinemeyer / © New Netherland Museum

PREFACE

The magnificent Hudson River flows for 300 miles from Lake Tear of the Clouds in the Adirondack wilderness to New York Harbor—half estuary, half river. Half estuary because the tides from the ocean course up and down the river from New York City to Troy, roughly half its length, in a neverending cycle of ebb and flow; half river because fresh water flows down the river from its source in the mountains and from a multitude of smaller rivers, streams, and creeks that feed it along the way, eventually to meet the tides. That is why the Indians called it the "river that flows two ways."

Along the banks of this mighty river are many hidden coves, open bays, and shallow watery pools that are continually flooded and drained by the tides, creating large and small marshes, swamps, and wet meadows. As far north as Beacon, about sixty miles above New York Harbor, the tides that slosh up and down are salty or brackish. Farther north the tidal flow, diluted increasingly by fresh water, has lost its salinity, and fresh water only washes in and out of the coves, inlets, and bays between Beacon and Troy.

Many of the coves and bays have been further altered or speeded in their slow transition to marsh or swamp by the causeway of the railroad that was built almost 150 years ago along the east bank of the river. The tidal water flows into the wetlands through railroad bridges and culverts. It is to one of these fresh-water tidal bays near my home that I am drawn repeatedly with my notebook and camera to try to learn its secrets, to record in words and photographs its beauty, its magic, and its ecological significance.

The great marshland that I have been exploring for several years is Tivoli North Bay and the adjacent Tivoli South Bay in Dutchess County on the east shore of the Hudson River. I was introduced to these bays in the 1970s by my biologist son, Erik, who was at the beginning of what has become his lifelong hands-on work and research on wetlands ecology in the Hudson River Valley and elsewhere.

The Tivoli Bays area stretches for about three miles from the village of Tivoli south to Barrytown. Part of the protected Hudson River National Estuarine Research Reserve, this magnificent wetland is governed by the fresh water tides which flow in and out twice daily, creating a constantly changing land and waterscape and a diverse habitat for myriad life forms.

The Research Reserve, established in 1982, is part of a nationwide network of estuarine areas, some salt, some fresh, created under the Coastal Zone Management Act. The protected area includes three

other distinct estuarine sites—Piermont Marsh and
Iona Island to the south, and Stockport Flats to the
north, connected by the great ribbon of the Hudson
River. Managed by the New York State Department
of Environmental Conservation, the Research
Reserve is a natural outdoor laboratory for scientists
and students, birdwatchers, hikers, canoeists, photog-
raphers, and anyone interested in being outdoors.
Additionally, Tivoli Bays is also a New York State
Wildlife Management Area, where hunting and fishing are enjoyed.

Like all tidal wetlands, Tivoli Bays is one of the
most biologically productive places on earth. In
these shallow watery worlds, fed by the changing
tides and nutrients from the land, aquatic plants
and algae flourish and decay, providing food and
shelter for hundreds of species of fish, reptiles,
insects, and other animals, including many fish
that feed us. Wetlands also filter and cleanse the
waters.

Getting to know this Research Reserve, with its
two large bays, two river islands, and the adjoining
uplands, 1700 acres in all, has not been easy. When
I first began to walk the perimeter of the wetlands
and later to explore its inner reaches by canoe, it
looked flat and uninteresting. Its impact on my
senses was subtle and gradual. It did not suddenly
arouse my sensibilities like the spectacular scenery
of western mountain ranges and canyons, or the
crashing waves of rocky ocean shores. It took a
while for its quiet grace to register on my heart and
my mind.

Before I could really appreciate the beauty and
mystery of the wetlands, I had to spend many
days—early mornings, high noons, and late evenings;
at high tides and low tides; in winter, summer, spring,
and fall—literally and figuratively immersed in it. I

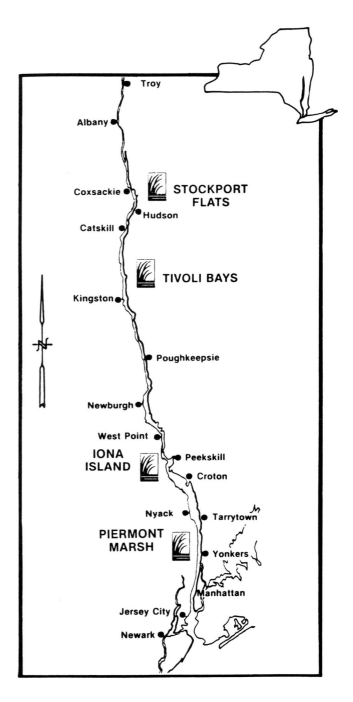

Hudson River National
Estuarine Research Reserve
Sites

have had to begin to know its history, prehistory, and natural history, its relationship to the forested uplands to the east of it and the great river to the west of it, and most of all, its relationship to mankind.

"In nature, one never really sees a thing for the first time until one has seen it for the fiftieth," wrote Joseph Wood Krutch in *The Desert Year.* "It never means much until it has become part of some general configuration, until it has become not a 'view' . . . but an integrated world of which one is a part . . ."[1]

And so I return again and again, carefully walking the rough edges in winter, carrying my photo equipment through ice and snow, sticky muck, and tidal water, sometimes knee deep; sauntering more slowly in spring as I savor the returning warmth and emerging creatures and vegetation. Most rewarding of all are the times from late spring to fall when I can explore and photograph the wetland wonders from my canoe, paddling slowly between the walls of hypnotically swaying cattails, or pulling over and resting in a hidden cove among the ancient-looking marsh plants and letting the marsh tell me about itself—whirring insects, birds singing their melodic songs, a muskrat slipping off the muddy bank with a splash, an elegant blue heron flapping overhead, a mother duck and her babies hiding in the cattails.

Little by little, I have begun to know some of the secrets of the marsh, but as many times as I visit it, it always retains its mystery and its magic, and surrounds and soothes me with its solitude and wildness.

The gently moving water, the waving cattails, the sighing wind, the gauzy veil of early morning mists, the clear liquid chorus of bird sounds, the rhythm of rising and falling tides—all these things become part of me and I am an infinitesimal part of them.

Along the way, I have kept an on-again, off-again journal of my nature observations, adventures, and musings on beauty, ecology, and how the rhythmic cycle of tides, days, months, and seasons of the wetland affect and synchronize with my own life rhythms. These notes, augmented by research and walks and talks with naturalists, along with the photographs I have taken over the past ten years, both black and white and color, form the basis for

The Hudson—half estuary, half river.

this book. It is my hope that in perusing it, you may be inspired to explore Tivoli Bays or other wetlands and natural places along the Hudson River, or at the least, as you read, you may experience some of the same solitude and wildness that I find when I go to the marsh.

Esther Kiviat

✿ ✿ ✿

"We need the tonic of wildness, to wade sometimes in marshes where the bittern and the meadowhen lurk, and hear the booming of the snipe; to smell the whispering sedge where only some wilder and more solitary fowl builds her nest, and the mink crawls with its belly close to the ground . . . We need to witness our own limits transgressed, and some life pasturing freely where we never wander."

Henry David Thoreau
Walden. 1854

ACKNOWLEDGEMENTS

Many persons have helped in the making of this book since the day in 1987 when I took my first photograph in Tivoli Bays—family, friends, scientists, artists, students, hunters, hikers, historians, and more. I owe them all a fervent thanks.

First, I am deeply indebted to my ecologist son, Erik, who shared with me his fascination for Tivoli Bays and his extensive knowledge of the area. He perused each chapter for scientific accuracy and has been a continued source of information, answering my constant questions and allowing me full use of his research studies, library, and all the resources of Hudsonia, Ltd. This book is his as well as mine.

My editor, Anita Wiener, read and reread the manuscript, from early drafts to final copy, suggesting needed changes and corrections and always offering gentle criticism and support.

From the earliest days, artist-designer Lucille C. Nickerson was my constant walking companion in the wetlands. This past year she has used her creative talents to help design the book.

Special thanks are due to the staff of the HRNERR: Betsy Blair, Reserve Manager, for her continued guidance and sponsorship; Dennis Mildner, Education Coordinator, for his time and knowledge as he canoed and hiked with me in marsh, swamp, and forest; Katherine Gould-Martin, Administrative Coordinator, and other staff members for assistance in numerous ways. Betsy and Dennis also served as readers.

Botanist Gretchen Stevens and ichthyologist Bob Schmidt of Hudsonia accompanied me on field excursions and reviewed pertinent chapters. Entomologist Kathleen A. Schmidt, who drew the attractive illustrations and the trail map, also reviewed sections on insects. John Winthrop Aldrich commented on historical text and contributed many suggestions and wrote the foreword. Annys Wilson, Bard College archivist, searched out reference materials; Barbara Bielenberg, president of the Egbert Benson Historical Society, helped locate old photographs. Middle school student Heather Kayal also read and commented on the manuscript, while conversations with Ricky Aldrich, Reid Bielenberg, John Carbury, Frank Dezago, Owen Kinery, and Donna Matthews enriched the text.

Thanks are owed to a host of assistants and volunteers, who carried equipment in the field, paddled the canoe, or kept me company as I photographed: Barth Anderson, Lorraine Costello, Ann Collins, Cheryl Griffith, Denise Edelson, Richard Edelson, Manos Kypraios, Joshua Miller, Stephanie Matteson, Gabrielle Myers, Rose Rahilly, among others.

Ron Linton introduced me to the mysteries of the computer, and he and Nicholas Westlund have put the book into computerized format. John

Porcella provided a computer. I have enjoyed working with my publisher, Wray Rominger of Purple Mountain Press, who has been encouraging and helpful as the book took shape.

I am especially grateful for the financial assistance provided by the following programs and foundations:

• Decentralization Program of the New York State Council on the Arts, administered by the Dutchess County Arts Council.

• Dutchess County Arts Fund Photographer's Fellowship
• Furthermore, the publication program of the J. M. Kaplan Fund
• Heritage Task Force for the Hudson River Valley, Inc.
• Hudson River Improvement Fund of the Hudson River Foundation for Science and Environmental Research
• The Thanks Be To Grandmother Winifred Foundation

❀ ❀ ❀

SPRING

In early April, the old winter cattails stand guard over the tide channel, new green shoots still hidden among the stalks.

The mottled hood of skunk cabbage, earliest of spring flowers, pokes
up through spongy mosses and dried oak leaves in the wetland.

Radiant marsh marigolds glowing in the tide swamp (above) and the fresh green of sunlit arrow arum (below) signal the advent of spring.

In late April and early May, elegant yellow iris blooms at the Stony Creek canoe landing, mingling with the

spring shoots of arrow arum and narrowleaf cattail against a panorama of distant mountains and cloud-filled sky.

After a chilly June night at a small marshy pond on Cruger Island (right), a giant bull-frog waits in the duckweed for the morning sun to warm its cold-blooded body (above).

A late March view from a bluff overlooking North Bay reveals meandering tide channels among the cattail banks.

I APRIL

Cattails
and
Catskills

The sun is just beginning to slant through the tall oaks and maples at the Stony Creek canoe landing above the marsh on this spring day in late April. The air is still nippy, but warm enough to venture out in a canoe for the first time this year, and so my friend Anne and I have taken the van with the red canoe on top to Tivoli North Bay for an exploratory paddle.

I am not only a novice marsh watcher, but also a novice at handling a canoe. In the early days of my Tivoli Bays project, my husband Charles patiently taught me how to handle the bow of the craft while he paddled stern or held the canoe steady as I photographed. When my marsh forays became more frequent, Charlie suggested that I find another companion for my safaris. For this trip I have enlisted Anne's help to paddle me around the wetlands.

We enter the Tivoli Bays National Estuarine Research Reserve at the brown and yellow sign of the New York State Department of Environmental Conservation (DEC) on Kidd Lane and drive slowly along through some of the forested uplands which buffer Tivoli North Bay. Down the road a once beautiful old barn, now sadly vandalized, tells us this heavily wooded area had been farmland. Virgin trees were cut for timber and land cleared for fields not too long ago. Renewing itself, the forest has grown back in less than a century with a rich mix of beech, oak, maple, tulip-trees, pine, and hemlock. A short distance beyond the barn, a sharp curve in the road brings us out on a bluff where the upland meets the marsh. The panorama of Tivoli North Bay is spread below us, visible through the still leafless branches of the hardwoods. Meandering channels of blue water, reflecting the blue of the sky, are lined with beigy-brown bands of cattails and other gray and brown and straw-colored vegetation. No outward signs of spring greening are visible from the bluff.

Through the open car window comes a pervasive sweet-spicy scent. "Spicebush," I tell Anne, pointing out a colony of shrubs on the hillside, their slender branches covered with thick clusters of tiny chartreuse-yellow flowers. One of the earliest of spring blooms, spicebush is also known as wild allspice. The bright aromatic red berries, which follow the flowers, were dried and ground and used as a substitute for

1

allspice in Revolutionary War times. Years ago, when I was conducting outdoor education programs for young children and teachers, we brewed its twigs and young leaves into a pleasant spicy tea. Growing in moist woods, spicebush is a common shrub around the wetland's edges. Wood and hermit thrushes and other birds will later feast on the fruits. Deer, opossums, and cottontails relish both fruit and twigs in fall.

Parking the van by the canoe landing, I take Anne for a brief detour into the nearby woods to see if a red trillium is in bloom. Last spring I had discovered one in a secret place just off the parking space. There it is, almost hidden in the underbrush, a perfect showy bloom about three inches across, surrounded by green fiddleheads of ferns. Three dark red petals, three red sepals, on a short slender stalk rising up above three large green, almost heart-shaped leaves. Three–three–three: all the parts are in threes. The red trillium is also known as wake robin, a name that always hints of spring to me.

Mindful of the tides, we do not linger in the woods. The Stony Creek canoe landing, the only boat access into North Bay from its eastern edge, is at the bottom of a steep embankment. Before unloading the canoe, we scramble down the path to check the water depth.

At the bottom is the simple wooden dock where we will put in our canoe. "Tidal Landing. Load and Unload at High Tide Only," ominously warns the sign on a nearby tree. According to the chart I consulted before planning the morning's adventure, high tide should be about 9:30 AM. We have about an hour and a half before high tide and an hour and a half afterwards to explore the marsh. If we return when the tide has moved inexorably out to the river, the shallow passage leading from the main channel to the dock becomes a mud flat and we could become mired in the sticky muck. Once, when I was just getting acquainted with the marsh and the supposedly predictable tides, I miscalculated and a companion and I found ourselves almost knee-deep in very wet mud that grabbed and pulled at our boots as we struggled to carry the canoe into shore.

Fortunately, a few years later the DEC built steps on the lower section of the slippery trail down the embankment, and more recently, installed a floating dock out to the Stony Creek channel. Now canoeists can put their craft directly into the water at any tide level.

Before these improvements were made, I had to learn how to interpret the tide table and take into account the vagaries of river currents, winds, and the phases of the moon. Although the chart says high tide is at 9:30 it could vary considerably. Published tide tables are only predictions based on past measurements. In calculating the tides for any given point along the river, the tables add a specific number of hours to the predicted time of the tide in New York Harbor, where the Hudson meets the sea. It takes a tidal flow starting at the mouth of the Hudson estuary six hours to make its slow way 100 miles northward to Tivoli Bays.

Experiences at the canoe landing and along the Cruger Island causeway, where marsh walkers have to cross a tidal flow to get to Cruger Island, have taught me not to trust the tables. Tidal times may vary by as much as forty-five minutes from the stated times. Periods of abnormally high or low barometric pressure, continual north or south winds, or a few days of heavy rains—all can alter the time of the tides. A major storm might throw tidal calculations off by as much as an hour and a half.

Tides have their own terminology: a northbound current is a flood current or tide; a southbound current is an ebb tide; between the flood and the ebb is a brief time known as the slack tide, when the current pauses before changing directions. Spring tides are not high tides in the spring of the year, but unusually high tides springing up over the normal tide heights. They occur from time to time throughout the year, due to a combination of circumstances. For instance, if the moon is full or new and also at perigee, that is, closest to the earth when its gravitational pull is strongest, an abnormally high tide might occur. The average range of the tides in the Hudson River at Tivoli Bays is four feet. The tides flood into North and South Bay under five railroad bridges.

The one constant I have learned as I try to figure out when the tide will be most advantageous for my marsh explorations, whether on foot or by canoe, is that the estuarine tides slosh in and out of the wetlands approximately every twelve hours, in a never-ending cycle of ebb and flood.

A tide channel provides a watery highway through Tivoli North Bay.

Graceful mute swans take off in tandem over a raft of spatterdock.

Now Anne and I can see the tide coming quietly in, the movement barely discernible near the canoe landing. The water is already ten inches deep at the dock, ample depth to launch our canoe without stepping in the thick black ooze. The rising water is lapping at the gnarled roots of the old beech tree hanging near the landing. Some coppery brown leaves still cling to its branches, while the elongated buds are already swelling with tiny new spring leaves ready to burst out. The constant surge of the tides has undercut the bank and exposed the roots of the beech. How long will it be, I wonder, before the old tree, clinging tenaciously to the bank, will topple into the tides.

Back up the short steep path, Anne and I struggle to ease the canoe off the top of the high van. Fortunately, Anne is almost six feet tall, a handy height for unloading the craft. She is a good counterpoint to my five feet two. We lower the canoe to the ground, carry it down the slippery slope to the dock, and place it in the water.

A canoe is the ideal craft for exploring a swamp, a bog, or a marshland. With its shallow draft, it can slip smoothly and noiselessly through as little as six inches of water, causing a minimum of disturbance for observing wildlife. Paddling rhythmically in the flat water of a marsh is relaxing and almost effortless, except for those times when a sudden wind comes up and blows wildly across the wetland. Even a novice like me can guide the slim boat easily through the cattails and reeds to investigate small secret coves and hidden tidal pools. My fiberglass canoe is only fifteen feet long and weighs just fifty-five pounds—about as much weight as a little old lady in tennis shoes can handle, with help, to lift and carry it down and back. It has a flattish bottom and is amazingly stable, important as I twist and turn or lean over the side, or stand up occasionally to get a photo shot of an out-of-reach flower or a bird's nest high up in the cattails.

In The Wind in the Willows, Kenneth Grahame's beloved book, Water Rat says: "There is nothing–absolutely nothing–half so much worth doing as simply messing about in boats; simply messing . . . about in boats."[1]

As we paddle out through the narrow canoe trail toward a wide tidal channel just offshore, we savor the quiet beauty of the scene. A tangle of emergent plants stands near the shore–wild yellow iris, just starting to bloom; tall dried stalks of last year's cattails, standing like an army of straw men at the edge of the water; new shoots of arrow arum, arrowhead, and pickerelweed, three common marsh plants, all with vivid spring-green arrow-shaped leaves. These three plants were confusing at first for a new marsh watcher, until I learned to distinguish the subtle difference in their leaves.

A floating-leaved plant with large shiny heart-shaped leaves, the spatterdock, or yellow water-lily, partially fills the big offshore channel with its early growth. Opposite the shore a high bank borders the wider channel. It is edged by the ubiquitous cattails, their feet in the water, their dry stems and leaves stiffly erect. Above the cattails the bank supports a thick cover of shrubs and a few trees, obscuring the view of the rest of Tivoli North Bay, which stretches west to the Hudson River. Between the marsh and the river is the causeway of the railroad, also unseen. Rising up forty miles to the west, beyond the river, are the distant shadowy peaks of the Catskill Mountains, still covered with a smoky gray morning haze. The softly rounded ancient mountains watch broodingly over the river and the marsh. It is a typical North Bay scene: horizontal bands of tidal water, a band of cattails, a broad stretch of trees and shrubs, and above all, the misty Catskills, a scene that will be repeated often as we explore.

We stop paddling to photograph a brilliant yellow iris, shining like gold in the morning sun. The showy flowers are arranged in a plan of threes, three boldly-veined petal-like sepals arching down, three erect petals, and three prominent styles–the stalks of the pistils–which look like shorter petals over the sepals. Here again is that mysterious combination of threes in nature, which also occurs in the trillium. Why three? Nature has many mysteries, and we who come to watch and study its wonders, cannot fathom the why, nor is there any need to. It is enough to marvel at the beauty of the threes in the iris; the trillium; the flowers of the broadleaf arrowhead; the delicate lavender, white, or pink-petaled hepatica with its three-lobed leaves; and countless other flowers.

A canoe is the ideal craft for exploring a marsh.

Golden petals of a wild yellow iris light up the wetland edges.

The iris petals are irregular, those of the trillium symmetrical; iris sepals, petals, and styles are all a radiant yellow. The leaves of the iris are slender and sword-shaped, like cattail leaves, but branching gracefully out from the stalk, as well as rising from the base.

This lovely yellow iris is an alien from Europe, an escape from Colonial gardens, which has become well established and now grows wild along the edges of ponds, streams, and marshes throughout the Northeast. I silently thank those gardeners who brought its golden beauty to our shores, although wetland biologists worry that this alien invader might spread too densely and threaten the native vegetation, which provides important food and shelter to many wetland dwellers.

Elsewhere in Tivoli Bays, in the early summer, I have observed a native iris, the tall delicate blue flag. At the canoe landing, only the yellow iris mingles with the other emergent marsh plants–those which grow near the shore, their roots in water, their stalks, leaves, and flowers reaching above the ever-changing tides.

As we paddle closer to the cattails, we notice new sword-like green leaves springing up. Already four feet tall, they are still partially hidden among the old stems and leaves. The new leaves will reach their full height of six to eight feet when spring slips into summer. Then the cattail borders of the tide channels will take on their more familiar appearance: rippling, undulating walls of olive-green, glistening as they twist and turn in the winds, the trademark of Tivoli North Bay.

Consulting my field guides back home, I find that there are two kinds of cattails–narrowleaf cattail and broadleaf cattail, also known by many other picturesque names: flags, rushes, candlewicks, bulrushes, Cossack's asparagus, cat-o-nine tails,

cattail flags. The species which grows so abundantly in North Bay is the narrowleaf cattail.

In April its brown and tan sausage-like seed heads are shaggy and bedraggled after the winter's onslaught of wind and snow, but many millions of minute seeds, each with a tiny feathery plume, still cling to the spike. Anne and I watch entranced as countless bits of tan fluff, torn from the cattails by the wind, float on the water around our canoe, every cottony wad harboring hundreds more seeds. They swirl and slosh in the gentle current, like tiny water babies being rocked in the cradle of the wetland mother. They make abstract patterns, in sync with the rhythm of the tides, like everything else in this estuarine wonderland.

A single cattail spike produces a quarter-million seeds! I can't begin to calculate how many billion

An ecologist studies beetles on iris petals.

seeds are produced annually in this wetland. Only a few will survive, but nature has miraculously provided billions to ensure the survival of some.

Windblown or waterborne by the tides, the seeds may travel miles. One may come to rest on a favorable spot of mud and begin to grow. The new young cattail plant thus produced puts out a creeping rootstock, which grows in all directions and produces new leaves at close intervals, so that in a year or two each plant becomes the center of a kingdom of cattails. Environmental conditions in Tivoli Bay were undoubtedly very favorable to the growth of cattails, and so, cloning themselves (without the aid of genetic scientists!), they proliferated and became the dominant plant in this fresh-water tidal marsh.

North Bay consists of about 200 acres of mostly cattail and 150 acres of tree and shrub swamp, purple loosestrife, spatterdock, and open water. In contrast, Tivoli South Bay, the adjacent tidal bay, has very few cattails. It is larger, shallower, and more open.[2]

Cattails are a valuable source of food and shelter for many species of wildlife. Only a few birds feed on its minute hairy seeds, but geese, ducks, and muskrats relish the starchy rootstocks. The red-winged blackbird and several other species of birds nest and roost in its protective stalks. For some, such as the little marsh wren, the least bittern, and the common moorhen, it is the major nesting

Least bittern

habitat in North Bay. Numerous insects live on the cattail and find winter shelter in its stalks, roots, and fruits.

Many parts of the cattail are also utilized by people. Native Americans used the dried stalks to make mats and bags. They mixed the down with animal fat and used it medicinally to make a poultice for sores and injuries. The leaves have traditionally been used to weave natural rush seats and backs for chairs. Young flower spikes can be peeled, boiled, and eaten like corn-on-the-cob; the tender green shoots in early spring cooked like asparagus; and the sweet starchy roots eaten raw, baked, roasted, or boiled. Camping with a group of children many years ago, I helped them make some fine golden flour from the yellow pollen, shaking it from the flower spikes, then mixing it with whole wheat flour, baking powder, and water to bake pancakes on an old iron griddle over our campfire. No pancakes from a store-bought mix ever tasted so delicious.[3]

Of great importance to humans, cattails and other wetland plants act as a water purifier, a kind of natural sewage treatment plant. They use some pollutants as nutrients, absorbing nitrogen and phosphorus from human sewage, animal feces, and agricultural runoff, and return usable organic matter to the marsh when they die.

Out in mid-channel our canoe glides past the great raft of spatterdock. The heart-shaped leaves, folded over at the midrib, rise up out of the smooth surface of the water like giant rabbit ears. In early spring, before they have been discovered by the insects, the leaves are pure lustrous green, glistening in the sun. By midsummer they have become hatcheries for hordes of tiny water-lily leaf beetle larvae. Even now the parent beetles are laying their eggs on the ample pads. By the end of July, the leaves are riddled with tiny holes. They turn dull and yellowish, and are often coated with mud from the twice-daily dunking in the tides. Spatterdock has a deep yellow cup-shaped flower with a striking maroon-red center that you can see only if you look deep inside the cup. The flowering begins in June and continues through the summer.

Paddling past the spatterdock and around a bend, we lose sight of the shore and find ourselves in another world. It is a secret world, surrounded by walls of cattails that shut out all but the azure sky. We move silently through a labyrinth of narrow channels and passageways, like a maze, so that we don't know if we have been here before. Some of the channels are dead ends, some are meandering, some straight, some narrow, some wide.

At first it seems unusually quiet, but soon the subtle sounds, sights, and smells of the marsh begin to invade our senses. A black duck explodes from the water at our approach. A jaunty red-winged blackbird flies overhead and perches on a loosestrife twig, singing loudly. A distant honking directs our gaze westward to a flock of geese flying high over the river. From the shallows in a little cove where it had been fishing serenely, a great blue heron with a six-foot wingspread suddenly flaps up in front of our canoe and flies slowly off to another more private part of North Bay. Nearby we hear the reedy gurgling song of an unseen tiny marsh wren, a lovely song that to me is the voice of the marsh in spring. Rare in other parts of our region, the wren is a common dweller in Tivoli Bays.

A series of sharp whistles suddenly draws our gaze upward. A large bird, whitish underneath with black wing tips, is soaring overhead. Its white head and size suggest a bald eagle, but a crook in its great wings as it flies identifies it as an osprey, a fish-eating hawk. An eagle flies with flat wings, distinguishing it from an osprey even at great distances.

Red-winged blackbird perches on a cattail spike.

The osprey's story is a successful one, as research and conservation efforts have brought this magnificent raptor back from the brink of extinction in the last few decades. Because of its dependency on live fish as prey, the osprey was devastated by DDT contamination of aquatic systems and the fish that live in them. The DDT caused thinning of the osprey's egg shells so that the young did not survive. Today the great bird is a common spring migrant along the Hudson.

Toward the end of April and in early May, migratory ospreys gather over the tidal bays and creeks in our reach of the Hudson. They are attracted to the area by an interesting phenomenon, the annual spring spawning run of alewives. About the time of the vernal equinox, thousands of these curiously-named members of the herring family travel upriver a hundred miles or more from the ocean to lay their eggs in fresh water.

Known as "anadromous" fish, alewives grow up in salt water. When they are three or four years of age, they leave the ocean and swim up estuaries like the Hudson to spawn, then return to salt water. Their opposites, the eels, are known as "catadromous." The only catadromous species in the eastern United States, eels live in fresh water like Tivoli Bays and travel downriver to the ocean to lay their eggs.

It is a spectacular sight to witness a keen-sighted osprey circle on its powerful wings about seventy-five feet above the shallows of the bay or a tidal creek, then suddenly dive straight down, plunging feet first into the water, and come up with a silvery ten or twelve-inch fish in its curved beak. For the past few years I have been privileged to witness this thrilling sight on an an annual spring canoe trip led by Dennis Mildner, education coordinator for the Hudson River National Estuarine Research Reserve.

Observing the abundant life all around me on this late April day, I am beginning to understand how

Spatterdock (yellow water-lily) is a common wetland plant.

tidal marshes like Tivoli Bays are among the most productive places on earth and serve as nurseries for thousands of species. Nutrients and plant debris tumble down from the nearby uplands on the east and wash in on the tides from the river on the west. Settling to the bottom in the warm shallow waters, they mix with the detritus, the decaying matter from dying marsh plants, creating a rich environment where microscopic plankton such as algae, minute crustaceans, and other invertebrates, along with aquatic plants, flourish.

Tiny fish, such as killifish, pick their food off the bottom and off plants and surface film. Red-winged blackbirds, ducks, geese, bitterns, eels, bigger fish, snapping turtles, muskrats, and other marsh inhabitants in turn eat the killifish or plants and seeds or both. Some of the bigger fish become potential food for man as well as for other predatory animals. The predator at the top of the chain in Tivoli North Bay, the snapping turtle, may in turn be eaten by man, although the New York State Department of Health now warns against the consumption of snappers, which are loaded with toxic polychlorinated biphenyls (PCBs).

Cattails, arrow arum, pickerelweed (emergent plants); spatterdock and duckweed (floating plants); wild-celery and pondweeds (underwater plants) grow and die. Birds, turtles and fish, beetles and dragonflies, and countless other creatures of the fresh-water wetlands breed and lay their eggs, and living and dying, return nutrients to the marsh, while the ever-changing tides carry riches back into the river-estuary.

By mid-morning, Anne and I have paddled slowly across North Bay to its western shore against the railroad embankment. Suddenly an Amtrak turbo train comes roaring along the tracks, shattering the silence and momentarily breaking the spell that the solitude and wildness of the marsh has cast over us. Brought back to reality, we notice that the tide has reversed and is flowing swiftly out of the bay, under the railroad bridge, and back again into the Hudson River, where it will once more make its six-hour trip down 100 scenic miles to New York Harbor and the endless seas beyond.

The tide ebbs and flows so imperceptibly that you can scarcely see the movement unless you are near an inlet such as the railroad bridge. Anne remarks contemplatively that the tide is a lot like growing older. "You don't always notice the passing years until suddenly you see a major change," she says. I agree with her somewhat, although now that I am in my eighth decade, the passage of time becomes much more obvious than the gentle changes of the tides. The rhythm of my life seems to be speeding up at this stage, instead of changing gradually and intangibly.

The ebbing tide tells us it is time to head back east to the canoe landing. As we paddle against the outgoing tide, a sudden wind begins to blow. The calm waters are now ruffled. The birds are momentarily silent. The heron has disappeared. The cattails, stiff and old from their winter sojourn, still stand guard. Paddling is becoming more difficult as we hasten to get back before the outgoing tide leaves us stranded in the mud, and we are keenly aware that the estuarine marsh is a place of constant change.

Horizontal bands of water, cattails, trees, and the misty Catskills create a typical landscape in North Bay.

Like gold-encrusted fingers rising from the tidal mud, the lovely golden club, rare elsewhere in the region, grows profusely in a small tidal marsh off of Cruger Island.

2 MAY

In Pursuit of the Golden Club

A delicate golden torch on a naked thick white stalk, curving gently upward and outward from a sheath of slender oval leaves—that is the golden club, a flower of striking beauty. A rare plant in New York State, it grows in only a few places along the Hudson River, including a secluded habitat in the Tivoli Bays. Here, despite its disappearance or apparent decline in many of the places in our region where it was once abundant, it seems to thrive.

One day in mid-May, when it is normally in bloom, I plan to search for the golden club. It grows in a small tidal marsh off Cruger Island. If the tides are right, it should not be too difficult to find. Low tide will be the most favorable time to reveal this flowering rarity, as it is partially immersed when the tides are high.

I had encountered it previously in the Okefenokee Swamp on the border of southern Georgia and Florida, where the golden club grows profusely, not knowing then that it could be found in the Hudson River close to my home.

Today's expedition to find this elusive plant will be on foot rather than by canoe, with my constant walking companion, Lucille Nickerson. To get to the hidden habitat of the golden club, we will walk out Cruger Island Road from the Bard College campus, following it west through wooded uplands for about a half-mile, and then through the narrow strip of tidal swamp known as the Neck, to the railroad tracks along the Hudson River. This swamp is the boundary between the open waters of Tivoli South Bay and the more closed cattail wetlands of Tivoli North Bay. Across the railroad a trail continues onto the off-shore island, which after many years has become a kind of peninsula connected to the mainland by sedimentation.

Cruger Island Road, where it runs through the swamp, is in reality a causeway between the mainland and the island, built sometime prior to 1835 to provide a thoroughfare for visitors to the enchanting island.[1] A reasonably firm footing for marsh walkers is still provided by the causeway. Before it was constructed, this area was probably a swampy wetland between North and South Bay. The causeway no doubt precipitated a greater distinction between the bays and gave us the dividing line we use today.

Hooded sheaths of skunk cabbage poke up through patches of snow.

As we search for the hidden golden club we will also discover and savor the delights of mid-spring along the Neck. The swamp is characterized by woody plants—a tangle of trees and shrubs and snags, along with herbaceous (soft-stemmed) plants, in the tide creeks on either side of the road.

We walk slowly through the shady pine, hemlock, and oaks along the first part of Cruger Island Road, noting the spring greening of the forest. White clouds of shadbush are in bloom, and tiny new leaves have unfurled on the deciduous trees and shrubs. Farther along are some fallen and decaying logs, covered with a luxuriant velvety cushion of mosses and lichens. The moss-covered logs serve as moist nurseries for the seeds and spores that fall upon them, and every down trunk displays miniature colonies of plants. There are several kinds of bright green mosses, from which sprout a Lilliputian forest of fragile thread-like stalks, each bearing a spore capsule like a tiny flag at its tip. Gray-green lichens

are scattered among the mosses, with here and there graceful curving fronds of young ferns or a seedling of an unidentified flowering plant. Each fallen trunk, as it decays, is giving birth to new life in this swampy environment.

A sign on a tree warning that the road beyond is tidal tells us that we have arrived at the beginning of the Neck. We know from past experience that here the road is often flooded, calling for knee-high waterproof boots, or at the least, old sneakers for slogging through the mud and water. Luckily, the tide is low this morning and there are only some ankle-high puddles.

Alongside the path, in a watery hollow, a bright emerald patch of gigantic skunk cabbage leaves, some as long as two feet, lights up the swamp. This wetland plant flowered in late winter before its leaves unfurled. Then its attractive purple-brown hooded spathe, mottled with yellow, poked bravely up through patches of snow and ice. Also known as meadow cabbage and devil's tobacco, its common name of skunk cabbage derives from the foul odor of the leaves when crushed. A young child once remarked that he thought skunks ate it like cabbage. Not so, I told him, letting him get a whiff of the strong odor. Any skunk or other creature attempting to eat the cabbage-like leaf would get a mouthful of sharp oxalic acid crystals with which the foliage is endowed.

Despite its strong odor and inedibility, its huge leaves create an aura of buoyant spring in the muddy swamp and lend a kind of primitive feeling to the scene, a feeling that I always have when I wander in the swamp.

Another strange and truly primitive plant, the horsetail, flourishes along the edge of the causeway. Mingling with pale lavender sticky geraniums and the golden globes of dandelions are foot-high stalks of horsetails, with feathery whorls of delicate green branches, looking like miniature pine trees. This morning the tiny tree-like structures are sparkling with dew. In April, the horsetails displayed bare bamboo-like jointed hollow stems, six to eight inches tall, each topped by a club-like cone or strobilus, which produces spores. Every cone is a tiny delight, with many hexagonal scales arranged in a close-fitting geometrical pattern.

Horsetails are allies of the ferns. Their ancestors lived about 250 million years ago in the immense primeval swamps of the Carboniferous Period. These ancient relatives of the horsetails on Cruger Island Road were towering trees, up to sixty feet high. As I contemplate this little plant in the Tivoli Bays swamp, I suddenly seem to shrink in size, until I am a mere speck in the history of the earth. I shiver as I look around me at the monstrous leaves of the skunk cabbage, the waist-high ferns, the horsetails, and the twelve-foot high giant reeds along the edge of the tide creek.

At that moment a huge creature sticks its head up out of the water and clambers onto the bank. I gasp. A second look reveals the beast to be a snapping turtle. I immediately resume my normal size and return to the present. The turtle, not long out of its winter hibernation in the mud on the bottom of the swamp, has a shell about fifteen inches long. As I move a little closer, it slips back into the swamp and disappears under the dark water.

A loud hammering draws my gaze upward. A gigantic black and white woodpecker with a spectacular red crest is poised on the trunk of a dead tree, boring loudly into the rotting wood in its search for insects. The swamp seems full of strange and over-sized species of plants and animals today. The woodpecker is crow-sized, almost twenty inches from the tip of its tail to the point of its crest. It is a pileated woodpecker. Other species of common woodpeckers in the wetlands, like the little downy and the slightly larger hairy woodpecker, are only about six to nine inches long. Uncommon in our area up to a few years ago, pileated woodpeckers are now becoming more widespread. As large as it is, glimpses of the shy bird with its flaming red crest are infrequent. More often I find huge rectangular holes, up to three inches wide and sometimes a foot high, in the dead wood of old trees where this winged woodsman has bored. As Lu and I watch, the woodpecker takes flight on its great wings, and we can hear the loud rush of its wingbeats overhead as it disappears into the pale blue sky.

Farther along the Neck, we come across a clump of radiant golden flowers lying low in the murky water. They are marsh marigolds, resembling giant buttercups, with their five-petaled brilliant yellow blossoms nestled among heart-shaped deep green leaves. (The "petals" are really sepals.) Some years, blooming as early as April among a few melting patches of

Horsetails, primitive plants, flourish along the wet edges of the swamp.

snow, they call to mind Thoreau's description of the first signs of spring—"It is the summer beginning to show itself, like an old friend in the midst of winter."[2]

Marsh marigolds are also called cowslips and mare-blobs. They are common in swamps, marshes, and other wet places throughout the eastern half of the country. According to wild-food specialist Euell Gibbons, marigolds have had many medicinal applications and have been used for the treatment of warts, fits, dropsy, and anemia. The boiled greens of marsh marigold are highly nutritious, rich in vitamins. Rains have leached essential minerals for centuries from higher lands, depositing them in marshes and swamps where they are absorbed by the wetland plants.[3]

A host of other flowers are in bloom this month, creating a colorful tapestry along the wet edges of the road. Buttercups, violets, the tiny blossoms of blue-eyed grass, and gill-over-the-ground, also known as ground-ivy, mingle with the green of sensitive fern and the horsetails. Large clumps of yellow iris stand farther back, their roots in the water among the shiny new leaves of spatterdock, which are already large but still young and fresh-looking.

Almost hidden in the tall grass on the road's edge we come across a moisture-loving jack-in-the-pulpit, the "preacher" standing upright in his "pulpit," the leafy green sheath or spathe, striped in brown, arching gracefully over his head. The preacher is really a club-like spadix, a brown stalk with tiny flowers at its base. In autumn the spadix displays a cluster of scarlet berries. Then I like to think that the preacher is wearing a cardinal's robe. Jack-in-the-pulpit is one of my favorite flowers. Whenever I find one I am reminded of Georgia O'Keefe's striking

Virginia rail

series of oil paintings of this wetland plant, depicting its beauty in sinuous curves of rich green, purplish brown, and maroon.

Jack-in-the-pulpit, skunk cabbage, and arrow arum are members of the arum family, distinguished by a hooded spathe enclosing an upright spadix. All are found in close proximity in the Tivoli Bays wetlands. Golden club is also a member of the arum family.

A few hundred feet into the tidal swamp, Lu and I are confronted by a wide jumble of rocks and water, where the tide creek flows across the manmade causeway. The water is about a foot deep. The tide is still outgoing, flowing gently from North to South Bay, on its way back to the estuary-river. We pick our way carefully along the wet rocks, slipping occasionally, but without a mishap. On other occasions we have encountered considerably deeper water at this spot, but our timing is better today. If we arrive after an especially high tide, the entire trail through the swamp is a series of deep puddles, and we have to wade through them or detour around them on a narrow precarious strip of mud in the brush on the side of the causeway. High tide makes the trail to Cruger Island an adventurous walk, but going at low tide is always easier.

Traversing the causeway for another quarter-mile to the railroad embankment, Lu says she is beginning to feel like the U.S. Mail, except that today it's not "rain, nor sleet" but tide puddles and muck that do not deter us on our appointed rounds.

An orchestra of bird song provides a melodic background to the sloshing of our feet, and we revel in the sound of some familiar birds—the hoarse call of a red-winged blackbird, the high thin notes of a chickadee, some geese honking in the distance.

Neither Lu nor I are expert birders, but we recognize these calls, and identify a splendid pair of orioles in the treetops and several tiny yellow warblers. At the the railroad tracks, I see a familiar figure, Alice Jones, a long-time member of the Ralph Waterman Bird Club. Alice has been birding and exploring the Tivoli Bays area for many years. This morning she is par-

ticipating in a spring bird count, with this section of the wetlands her assigned territory. She gladly shares with us the list of birds that she has spotted in the first few hours: barn and tree swallows, white-eyed vireos, red-eyed vireos, white-crowned sparrows, lots of yellow warblers, several goldfinches, a redstart, an osprey, many chickadees, a yellowthroat, a wood

Jack-in-the-pulpit is among the moisture-loving spring flowers on the causeway.

The tiny marsh wren, rare elsewhere, thrives in Tivoli Bays.

duck, several bluebirds, numerous red-winged black-birds, catbirds, and orioles. She heard a Canada goose calling from South Bay and phoebes and car-dinals singing nearby. Before the day is over, I am sure that Alice will record many more species.

The Tivoli Bays-Cruger Island area is one of the best localities for bird watching in the Hudson Valley. Researchers and birders from near and far come to observe and study bird life here. During migration, the bays become a birdwatcher's paradise. Because the Hudson River is a major flyway, many birds stop over to rest and feed here in fall and spring, and a varied population stays all summer.

Like most wetlands, both North and South Bay offer a rich and varied banquet for the birds. In North Bay, wild-celery, seeds of wild rice and smartweeds, larvae of the cattail moth, the water-lily leaf beetle, snails, and killifish are among the food offerings. In contrast to the seasonal and daily visi-tors, only a limited number of birds nest in North

Bay. The constant rise and fall in water levels as the tides ebb and flood is a deterrent to ground nesters; only those species which nest in emergent plants like cattails, reeds, and loosestrife above the high tide line breed in the tidal marsh.

A study of breeding birds in 1989 found the nests of twelve species in the open marsh of North Bay: marsh wren, red-winged blackbird, American goldfinch, least bittern, Virginia rail, song sparrow, swamp sparrow, willow flycatcher, eastern kingbird, yellowthroat, yellow warbler, and mallard. Several of these nesters—the marsh wren, the bittern, and the rail—are rare in the region.[4]

South Bay is frequented by birds of open water and mudflats, such as gulls, diving ducks, and great blue herons. Some, like the herons, move back and forth between North and South Bay.

Leaving Alice to continue her bird count, we cross the railroad tracks with extreme caution. We are aware that Amtrak trains, which speed north and south throughout the day, approach swiftly and cannot be heard until a few seconds before they bear down on the spot where one is standing. Access to the right-of-way requires permission from the rail-road and is dangerous. As a result the DEC discourages crossing the tracks.

Beyond the tracks the trail onto Cruger Island soon becomes a pleasant path covered with a thick carpet of leathery brown oak leaves. Lu and I are now surrounded by a mature forest of tall trees, mostly hardwoods: gnarled oaks, maples, beeches, birches, occasionally a handsome tulip-tree. Just off the path an old sycamore with a massive trunk towers against the blue sky, its white branches, the bark peeled away, resembling bleached bones.

Reaching a small stream, we leave the trail to search for the marsh where the elusive golden club flourishes. Away from the path the forest is dense and dark, with a heavy understory of shrubs, vines, and fallen trees. We push through the underbrush, climbing over large down trunks, and skirting around an impenetrable thicket. The ground underfoot is damp. The smell of decaying leaves and twigs, seeds and feathers, carcasses of dead insects and other animals, broken limbs and assorted debris that constantly falls on the forest floor permeates the air. Assisted by earthworms, ants, spiders, and a host of microscopic plants and animals, the abundant litter is being converted into soil. New growth in this enriched ground is already evident in lush ferns and mosses under our feet, in tiny seedlings that have taken root under the towering parent trees, in young saplings reaching upward toward the sunlight.

Our progress through the woods is slow. We are beginning to wonder if we have turned off the trail too soon, when the marsh where the golden club grows comes into view. The tide is out, revealing an expanse of mud and shallow water with an abundant growth of spatterdock, arrow arum, and pickerel weed. Willow shrubs, their branches a bright spring yellow, grow along the edges. Farther out is a stand of large trees.

About twenty feet from shore is the treasure we are seeking! Gold encrusted fingers on heavy white stalks up to a foot high, the flowers of the golden club arch gracefully up out of the swamp. A number of the endangered plants are visible throughout this hidden marsh.

Erik Kiviat estimated the golden club population in Tivoli Bays at about 2000 to 2500 plants. This is a healthy number, considering that Kiviat found the plant extirpated or declining in many of fourteen stands where it was previously known in the Hudson River between Kingston and Nutten Hook (about twenty miles north of Tivoli Bays). Golden club's territory seems to be limited by brackish waters on the south and pollution on the north. Dumping of dredge spoil, industrialization with its accompanying pollution, and a garbage landfill are among some of the factors that may have led to the decline of golden club.[5]

As we contemplate the scene before us, a graceful small white heron flies directly over our heads, settling down in the water about 100 feet from shore. Aided by binoculars, I observe the black bill and black legs with yellow feet—"golden slippers"—the identifying marks of a snowy egret. It displays just a hint of breeding plumage, some recurved feathers on its back. This little white heron has a wingspread of about three feet. A larger white heron, the great egret, is also found in Tivoli Bays, easily recognized by its yellow bill, black legs and black feet, and its greater wingspread of four and a half feet. The more frequently seen great blue heron, which stands four feet tall, has a wingspread of six feet or more.

Stepping carefully into the marsh, we decide we can slosh through to the golden club. A little off-

Many birders come to observe and study bird life in the area.

Early vegetation is visible in the hidden marsh where golden club grows.

shore, I put one foot on what looks like a solid spot, but as I step forward, my foot suddenly plunges into the muck. Losing my balance, I sit down with a plop. What a muddy mess I am as I struggle to my feet! Balancing on one foot, I try to pull my other foot out, but I have nothing to hang on to and treacherous mud is all around. Finally I extricate my foot from the boot and the boot from the marsh.

Booted once more, I cautiously inch toward the gleaming golden club. Now there is no place to set up a tripod near this beautiful plant, but ingenious Lu scavenges some small branches and a board out of the marsh to give me a somewhat precarious platform. Lu and I and the camera all survive without further mishap, as I photograph this unique flower.

When I sought out the golden club in a recent May, the plants nearly filled the marsh right up to the shoreline, and I photographed them without getting my feet wet.

Walking back along the causeway from Cruger Island, we savor our experience. The golden club is a survivor, thriving in its relatively healthy protected habitat in Tivoli Bays, free from the effects of encroaching civilization.

Other rare, threatened, and endangered plants and animals also have been found in the Research Reserve. One of these, the endangered heartleaf plantain, grows in only one location in North Bay. Most gardeners are acquainted with a related plant, the common plantain, considered by many a pesky weed.

The attractive endangered heartleaf, with its large, broadly oval-shaped leaves and tall curving spikes of tiny whitish flowers, is "possibly the rarest North American plantain," according to botanists Steven Clements and Richard Mitchell, in an article in the *Newsletter of the New York Flora Association*. It is considered special because it has known uses as a food and a medicinal plant. They quote an herbalist of the Potawatomi tribe as describing the plant's use in "healing of burns and sore feet when a tea of the roots is drunk." The botanists state that the "heartleaf plantain holds more promise than most rare plants for possible use in new foods and medicines."[6]

Another endangered plant, last reported in Tivoli Bays in 1936, is the tiny creeping Nuthall's micranthemum, an obscure member of the figwort family. This is the only recorded appearance of this plant in New York State, and one of only twenty recorded locations in the world. It may still exist, concealed somewhere in these heavily vegetated tidal swamps, marshes, and uplands, although botanists have not seen it in decades.

Tivoli Bays harbors numerous other species that are endangered, threatened, rare, or of special concern, nationally or in New York State. Among them are birds like the bald eagle, osprey, least bittern, peregrine falcon, and plants like ovate spikerush, Parker's pipewort, Eaton's bur-marigold, and estuary beggar-tick.

As we walk slowly back along the causeway from Cruger Island after our rewarding search for the golden club, we wonder how many other imperiled plants and animals may lurk in the swamps, marshes, and forests of this wildland. Known or still undiscovered, they need to be protected, not only because of possible medical, food, or other valuable uses, but to maintain diversity of species and to preserve the beauty and wonders of this special place for our own enjoyment and for our children and our children's children.

More than that, these species deserve to be helped to survive not only for what they can provide for humankind, but for their own sake. They are, after all, the true inhabitants of the wetlands.

❁ ❁ ❁

Save the Forever Wild

The point of all this
Is not, as you say
To save this
For future generations
Our children

This is too egocentric

The gopher
The blade of grass
The rock and the flea
Every piece of earth perched
On a ledge
And all life upon it
Is sacred
Whether we are here to appreciate it
Or not

This land is wilderness
To humans

It's home to everything else.

David Marell
UpRiver/DownRiver
Jan./Feb. 1991

Amtrak trains come roaring down the tracks no more than fifteen feet from the strip of soft soil where snapping turtles lay their eggs in June.

A female common snapping turtle with a twelve-inch shell digs her nest on the railroad causeway bordering Tivoli North Bay.

3 JUNE

Consider the Turtle

"Consider the turtle. A whole summer–June, July, and August–is not too good nor too much to hatch a turtle in. Perchance you have worried, despaired of the world, meditated the end of life and all things seem rushing to destruction; but nature has steadily and serenely advanced with the turtle's pace. The young turtle spends its infancy within its shell. It gets experience and learns the ways of the world through that wall. While it rests warily on the edge of its hole, rash schemes are undertaken by men and fail. Has not the tortoise learned the true value of time? You go to India and back and the turtle eggs in your field are still unhatched. French empires rise or fall, but the turtle has developed only so fast. So is the turtle developed, fitted to endure, for he outlives twenty French dynasties. One turtle knows several Napoleons, has seen no berries, had no cares, yet has not the great world existed as much as for you? What's a summer? Time for a turtle's eggs to hatch."

Henry David Thoreau
Journal, August 28, 1856

Red-winged blackbirds call from the cattails and reeds. A marsh wren sings its melodious song from a loosestrife twig near its nest. A big-beaked kingfisher, wearing a clerical collar, chatters from the telephone wires, preparatory to making a swift plunge into the water for a fish. Two mute swans fly overhead in tandem, their long necks outstretched, their wingbeats making a swishing sound. Sparkling drops of water on the fuzzy gray-green rosette of a mullein at my feet are reminders of last night's rain. Spring is a time of constant sound and movement in the marsh.

On this special day in early June, I am walking slowly along the railroad causeway that separates the tidal wetlands of Tivoli North Bay from the eastern bank of the Hudson River, looking for a strange Brobdingnagian creature. Almost on clue, there is a movement in the shrubby willows and silky dogwood that line the marsh edge, and a prehistoric relic with an armored shell and a massive head climbs up the bank out of the sticky black marsh mud, lumbers through the brush, and moves ponderously onto the cleared strip of bulky stones, cinders, and soft soil alongside the railroad tracks.

This hulking creature is a female snapping turtle. She is searching for a suitable nesting site where she may deposit the dozens of eggs already formed inside her enormous body, just as her ancestors before her have done every spring for more than two hundred million years.

This is the day I have been waiting for—my first opportunity to make the close acquaintance of this unlovely, much maligned wetlands creature. In the next few weeks and in each successive June for several years thereafter, I will observe and photograph dozens more nesting females, one of my most fascinating marsh experiences.

The narrow strip of black cinders and soil on the east side of the railroad causeway is a favored nesting place for the turtles of Tivoli North Bay, and it is here that I am privileged to watch this ancient ritual at daybreak.

As this great creature moves warily up the bank and onto the cinders, I am reminded once again of the long-ago beginnings of marshes and swamps. When the earth's first land creatures came up out of the sea, it was in the half-wet, half-dry world of the primordial marshlands.

The Tivoli Bays wetlands, to me, are still a primeval and mysterious place, with monstrous turtles, huge woodpeckers, and ancient-looking plants like ferns and horsetails, sedges and cattails. Looking out over the marsh at low tide, I imagine a gigantic dinosaur lumbering about in the muck while colossal armored turtles search for nesting sites. Similar turtles were on earth long before the dinosaurs. They witnessed the rise and fall of the "terrible lizards" and have come down through the eons essentially unchanged from the first turtles in the world.

"Consider the turtle,"[1] wrote Thoreau in his journal, and surely many have pondered the mysteries of this ancient beast and tried to fathom how it has survived and why it has long been a sacred and revered object in the myths and folklore of primitive peoples.

A prehistoric relic climbs out of the marsh in search of a nesting site.

An Iroquois creation myth depicts the Great Turtle as supporting the earth. A plaque in the Iroquois Indian Museum at Howes Cave, New York, tells the story:

> "In the Sky World was a longhouse. A tree with white blossoms grew in front of the longhouse. When the Chief of the Sky World uprooted the tree with the white blossoms, he created a hole in the Sky World. His wife fell through the hole. Ducks and geese caught her in their wings. The ducks and geese brought Sky Woman to sit on the back of a great snapping turtle. A muskrat brought mud from the bottom of the ocean and placed it on the back of the turtle. Earth grew on the turtle's back. We now live on Turtle Island."

The Iroquois Creation Story.

Southwest native peoples still use turtle shells as rattles in their sacred dances; Mexican Indians revered turtles as gods of fertility and rain. Most of us have heard some version of the Cherokee myth of the race between the turtle and an animal such as a rabbit, fox, or owl, in which the slow turtle outwits the faster animals by stationing his identical relatives at the top of seven ridges. When rabbit, fox, or owl arrive, turtle is already there.

A few years ago I saw an exhibit on humor in Japanese book illustration at the British Museum. In an old book, the *Bumpogafu* by Kawamuro Bumpo (1807), there was a sketch of Fukurokuju, God of Long Life and Happiness, with his legendary long-haired tortoise, considered the symbol of longevity to the Japanese. The illustration looked a lot like a snapping turtle, except that it had extremely long hair streaming down from around the edge of its upper shell. The Chinese also revered the turtle as the symbol of longevity.

Many epithets have been used to describe the uncomely snapping turtle: Old Ugly, Monster of the Marsh, Old Mossback, Horny Nightmare, Wickedest Critter in the Water, Gothic Gargoyle, among others. The common snapping turtle, the species inhabiting Tivoli Bays, is almost ubiquitous in waters east of the Rockies. It ranges from Canada southward through the United States, eastern Mexico, and parts of Central America to Ecuador. Its habitat is any body of water large enough and permanent enough to support a growth of aquatic plants. Although it prefers sluggish water with a muddy bottom, it may live in ponds, streams, rivers, swamps, and marshes, either fresh or slightly brackish.

Turtles are reptiles, related to snakes and lizards, alligators and crocodiles. They are "cold-blooded" creatures, that is, their body temperature is about the same as the water, earth, or air around them. There are about 250 kinds of turtles in the world today, and most of them occur in the United States and Canada. Only a few other species of turtles are known to inhabit the Tivoli Bays along with the snapping turtle: the painted turtle, the wood turtle, and the map turtle. These three are considerably smaller than the massive snapper and are found in smaller numbers. Diamond back terrapins, related to the map turtle, are found in brackish waters of the lower Hudson. Their home territory is the Atlantic Coast.

On my travels in Tivoli Bays I have observed

Painted turtle, one of three turtle species, in addition to the snapper, inhabiting Tivoli Bays.

it hibernates in bottom muck or occasionally on land; in spring it is usually found in water. Because it is partly terrestrial, it is vulnerable to destruction, especially by autos and people. This turtle is currently protected by state law.

Painted turtles, little reptiles about six inches long, are very common in the Northeast, especially in farm ponds and marshes. Easily recognized, they have red and black markings around the edge of the shell, bright black and yellow stripes on the head, and red stripes on the neck. A five-acre pond in Clinton Hollow, Dutchess County, where my husband and I directed a children's nature camp for thirty years, was well populated with these attractive little turtles. They were easily caught and well-loved by the campers. The pond also supported a number of large snappers.

Common snapping turtle was named *Chelydra serpentina* by Linnaeus, meaning "snakelike swampbeast." At first glance it bears little resemblance to a snake, but when threatened, it can strike like lightening, thrusting its head forward with its long snakelike neck to snap at an enemy with powerful jaws. It will grab a stick, a finger, a pants leg, or the appendage of a hapless animal and will not readily release its grip, probably the basis for tales about snapping turtles hanging on until sundown. Another myth about its powerful jaws is that it can sever an arm or a foot with a single crunch or snap off a piece of a broom handle. This fable was proved false when a biologist, Wilfred T. Neill, stuck a common lead pencil into the

painted turtles and seen them basking in the sun on logs or jetsam but have not yet encountered a map or wood turtle. The map turtle is so-called because of the map-like or ring-like patterns on the back of the young, although the pattern is obscure in adults. The head is marked with delicate yellow and blackish lines, yellow spots, and a light "mustache." The female may grow up to ten inches long, measuring its upper shell or carapace. (Scientists use length of carapace to indicate turtle size.) The female is much larger than the male. Map turtles nest and reproduce in the fresh water estuaries of the Hudson but are inconspicuous and hard to find.

The wood turtle has a brown "sculptured" carapace up to nine inches long. The lower shell, or plastron, is black and yellow. The throat and legs are marked with orange. The wood turtle is partly terrestrial and partly aquatic in habitat. In summer it ranges far from water, living strictly in woods and fields, but in fall it returns to swampy areas. In winter jaws of a large snapper. The reptile crushed the pencil but did not sever it.[2] A snapping turtle can bruise or lacerate a finger, but not bite it off!

The snapper becomes aggressive when it is threatened, probably because it has a very small undershell, the smallest of any species of turtle relative to its size, and the shell does not completely protect the turtle's body. Also this reptile cannot pull its fist-sized head fully into its armored shell, as most other kinds of turtles can.

The snapper's aggression occurs only on land. In water it is non-aggressive and docile except for catching food, or when a male engages in combat with another male to establish dominance, resulting in a very nasty and sometimes bloody fight. The turtle's moss-covered back and dark coloring camouflage it against the muddy marsh bottom, and it has few if any predators in the water. Often people are fearful of swimming in ponds inhabited by snappers, but they need not be. Erik Kiviat, who has conducted extensive research on turtles and has devoted more than twenty-five years to the study of snapping turtles, tells of a legendary turtleman, Jasz (pronounced "Yosh") Rodziewicz, whom he met a number of years ago when Jasz was harvesting turtles in Tivoli Bay. Jasz locates snappers underwater by feeling for them with his bare feet!

Needless to say, I maintain a proper distance from the great beast which has come ashore to lay her eggs. Her knobby dark brown upper shell is about twelve inches long and is covered with a dense growth of algae. Her hind legs are elephantine; her huge head has a hooked upper jaw which resembles a beak; her yellow-brown eyes are set close together. Like other turtles, she has no teeth, but her jaws are covered with a sharp-edged horny sheath. The long tail is armed with horny projections called tubercles, which resemble the ferocious-looking triangular armored plates along the back and tail of a mythical dragon or a Stegosaurus from the Jurassic Age.

The common snapping turtle grows to about twenty or thirty pounds, and its carapace may measure up to eighteen-and-a-half inches in length. Stories about two- to three-foot snapping turtles that live to a hundred years are myths–part of the mystique that surrounds this mysterious monster. The largest snapping turtle recorded in Tivoli North Bay weighed forty-four pounds and had an eighteen-inch carapace.

Occasionally a larger turtle may be found. In 1990, Bill Sherrod, a taxidermist, trapped a fifty-eight pound giant snapper in a small pond in Rhinebeck, where it had probably lived undisturbed for many years. Bill estimated its age at about fifty years. Despite its weight, its carapace measured only eighteen inches. Most of the nesting females I have observed in the past ten years range from nine to twelve inches long, with an occasional one up to fourteen inches. The males become much larger. The common snapper of Tivoli Bays has a close relative, the alligator snapping turtle of the lower Mississippi Valley and the Gulf Coast, that is truly Cyclopean. It is the largest fresh water turtle in the United States, averaging about a hundred pounds.

Another unfounded myth is that snapping turtles rapidly decimate any population of waterfowl in their marshy habitats, and that they are especially fond of tender young ducklings. It is true that snappers may devour some ducklings, an occasional bittern, or other birds, but analysis of stomach contents of *Chelydra* has shown that waterfowl are only a small percentage of its food intake. Snappers are omniverous–they eat anything organic that is available: water and

Map turtle

This hoary monster, found crossing a road, stares warily at the camera.

marsh plants; insects; snails, clams, and crayfish; eels, shiners, bullheads, and other fish; snakes, frogs, and toads; even small muskrats. The Tivoli Bay snappers consume large amounts of plant material, killifish, and fish carrion. Of great value in the tidal marshes is that they devour many dead animals, helping to keep the ecosystem in balance. They are the "garbage men" of the wetlands.

In the winter months, snappers hibernate in bottom muck, and possibly in muskrat bank dens and under old duck hunter's blinds, the haphazard, disintegrating structures which have been abandoned in the bays. Like other hibernators, their metabolism slows down and they need only small amounts of oxygen for survival.

An inch-long hatchling was found near the canoe launch in early fall.

The belief that turtles survive for hundreds of years is unfounded, although they are tenacious and long-lived. The length of their life exceeds that of any other backboned animal, including man. There is only one known longevity record considered accurate and that is of a turtle that lived at least 152 years. The best records of turtle age are from animals that have been in captivity, primarily in zoos.

Our local snappers may live to be fifty years old. With their protective armor and ferocious jaws, snappers are almost invincible. The heavy armored shell may be limiting–snapping turtles cannot glide like a snake, or climb trees. But the durable shell has proved its worth in protecting this species from predators over the eons.

Today the adult turtle's only enemy is man. Automobiles kill many, and snappers are harvested liberally for food. In the late sixties and early seventies, turtleman Rodziewicz reported taking two-and-a-half to three or more tons of snapper (about 300 to 350 individuals) annually out of Tivoli North Bay. However, when studies showed that Hudson River turtles carry heavy concentrations of PCBs and other contaminants in their bodies, they were no longer considered safe to eat, and Jasz has not harvested turtles in this area since then.

The extent of contamination in Hudson River turtles was determined by state pathologist Ward Stone through analysis of a number of turtles collected up and down the river. The studies revealed the turtles to have some of the highest levels of contaminants recorded from any wildlife anywhere in the state–possibly in the world. Most of the Hudson River snappers had muscle levels of PCB exceeding the two parts per million federal allowable limit in food. A few turtles had over 7,000 parts per million PCBs in their body fat![3]

Sadly, contamination of these snappers is a mirror of the pollution in the Hudson estuary. Snappers inhabit the mud of the wetlands which is permeated by toxic materials carried in constantly by the tides. Because these turtles are long-lived, they absorb great quantities of pollutants along with the food they eat over a period of many years.

Other creatures that live in the estuary or feed on aquatic vegetation, insects, and fish, also may have been affected by the PCBs dumped in the Hudson over several decades, primarily released by General Electric Company from their factory near Troy. The PCBs have been carried down the length of the river and have persisted in the mud, while a debate about how to eliminate them rages among federal and state governments, environmentalists, and General Electric.

The adult turtles of Tivoli Bays emerge from hibernation from mid-April to early May, when the alewives have come up the Hudson from the ocean in great numbers to spawn in the fresh-water estuary, and the tiny killifish have begun to feed again in the muddy shallows. Young turtles probably emerge later in May. Alewife and killifish become snapper's first

Dirt-speckled torn egg shells are all that remain of a nest destroyed by a predator. Raccoon tracks were found nearby.

food of the spring, while killifish and carp are basic summer foods, along with the great variety of vertebrates and invertebrates described above. The population of ducks and other marsh birds such as bitterns is not high enough in the bays in summer to make them a significant snapper food.

Like their ancestors, almost all species of turtles, whether aquatic or terrrestrial, have to lay their eggs on land. The snapping turtles in Tivoli North Bay seem to prefer the open strip of cinders and soil along the railroad embankment between the marsh and the river for nesting. The major requirements are that the nesting site be in a cleared area so that it receives an ample amount of direct sunlight for incubation of the eggs and that the soil be reasonably soft for digging.

Sometime between June 10 and 25, usually after a rain, dozens of the great creatures climb up the banks from the wetland ooze in this annual rite. Elsewhere *Chelydra* may travel up to a half mile from its home base in search of a suitable nesting site. It is at this time that many homeowners report the sightings of huge turtles lumbering across their lawns and digging in their gardens. Nest digging and egg laying usually take place in the early morning or early evening.

Today as I walk along the railroad causeway at the edge of the marsh I have the incredible good fortune to observe twenty-four nesting females. They are almost oblivious of my camera and me. They have climbed up out of the muck with a single-minded purpose, and nothing seems to deter them. They hardly even blink when trains roar down the tracks, scarcely fifteen feet away. Only once did I notice a reaction—a turtle I was photographing opened its mouth wide in terror or anger as a train sped past. Sometimes the slow-moving turtles try to cross the tracks and are killed by the trains. It is not known how many meet this fate. A few years ago I came across a dead turtle on the tracks, her body badly crushed by the speeding train, her eggs, fully formed, scattered about. The durable armored shell is no match for a steel behemoth.

Curiously, each snapper may dig several large shallow depressions, or body pits, before she finds a spot that is acceptable for her nest. She is a picky mother. Fascinated, I watch as one female colossus digs in the cinders with her hind feet, using them alternately, after first having shoved aside some large stones along the railroad right-of-way. Although I can't see under her posterior, she is hollowing out a bowl-shaped cavity about six to eight inches deep and about six inches wide at the bottom. In other locations, snapping turtles have been found to dig flask-shaped nests, but the cavities on the railroad causeway appear bowl-shaped, according to a Cornell University researcher who studied the nesting habits of *Chelydra* along the railroad embankment several years ago.[4]

When the hole is completed, she will deposit her eggs, about one a minute. The spherical white eggs, from twenty to fifty in a clutch, look like pingpong balls and have a tough leathery shell. Larger clutches—up to eighty-six eggs—ocasionally have been reported from other areas. When egg laying is completed, the snapper climbs off the nest, the black dirt falling off her body onto the eggs. Using her hind legs again, she "rakes" over the nest to conceal it;

Her posterior nearly buried, a female snapper is probably laying her eggs.

then, without a backward glance, she leaves her eggs to hatch from the warmth of the sun and returns to the cool waters of the tidal wetland.

Strange creature, I muse. Nothing deters her when it comes to digging a nest and laying her eggs, but she otherwise seems to have no parenting instinct. Turtles do not hatch their eggs, nor feed, care for, or protect their young. The nests are extremely subject to predation, and within a few nights to a few months, more than half the nests may be dug up by raccoons, skunks, foxes, coyotes, and other mammals. The tattered egg shells can be seen all along the railroad embankment.

The incubation period ranges from seventy to ninety days, possibly longer, depending on temperatures. The inch-long hatchlings, weighing about a half-ounce, emerge in late August or September. They peck their way out of the rubbery shell with an egg tooth, and laboriously dig upward through the soil and cinders covering their nest, a chore which may take as long as four days. Occasionally, if temperatures are unfavorable or the young cannot break out of the nest successfully, the hatchlings may overwinter in the nest, and the young turtles emerge in the spring (not observed at Tivoli Bays).

Baby snappers are perfect small editions of their parents, whom they will never know. Unerringly they make their precarious way toward the water of the marsh, some probably falling prey along the route to crows, gulls, raccoons, and other predators. In the water, little turtles also may be gobbled up by fish, frogs, herons, snakes, and even other turtles.

Little is known about the hatchlings once they reach the water. Young snapping turtles are not usually observed again until they are about five years old. We know, however, from the proliferation of turtles in Tivoli Bays and in other areas in the Hudson River Valley that many hatchlings survive and grow to Gargantuan adulthood to become as durable and invincible as their prehistoric ancestors. I am filled with admiration—even a fondness—for these remarkable reptiles. Surviving the depredations of marauding humans, other creatures, automobiles, trains, and man-made pollution, they will be, I am sure, the mighty rulers and guardians of the wetlands for many more millions of years.

A four-month-old juvenile snapping turtle in captivity.

The golden globes of spatterdock (yellow water lily), a common wetland plant, light up the bays from June to October.

Huge carp, one-and-a-half to two-and-a-half feet long, swim back
and forth in frenzied summer mating rituals at the edge of South Bay.

A bird watcher sits quietly in his canoe as early morning mist
hovers over North Bay. The Research Reserve is rich in bird life.

Many introduced species thrive in the Tivoli Bays, some displacing or threatening native species. Among the invaders are common reed with its tasseled plumes (left) and Queen Anne's lace and a Japanese beetle (below).

A researcher stands knee-deep in Eurasian water chestnut, an alien plant which carpets South Bay from June to September. It is a pest in the Northeast, spreading wildly at the expense of more valuable plants.

The "bonfires" of purple loosestrife, another invasive plant, spread through the wetlands, crowding out some native plants.

Nature awakens a sense of wonder in a young child. Purple loosestrife lines the edge of North Bay behind her.

Lavender spires of pickerelweed are backlighted by the sun. Great "meadows" of this native plant glorify North Bay in summer.

Brilliant scarlet cardinal flowers grow profusely around the shoreline of the bay in August.

Tall fronds of wild rice wave over the dense growth of water chestnut covering South Bay.

4 JULY

Water Chestnuts in My Sneakers

Low tide is predicted for about two thirty on this hot afternoon in early July. Robert Schmidt, a fish biologist, will be my guide today as we examine the vegetation in Tivoli South Bay.

We meet at the Bard College Ecology Field Station, which overlooks the bay, and descend a short rocky path to the water's edge. South Bay stretches out in front of us, a large open tidal inlet quite unlike its neighboring cove, Tivoli North Bay. North Bay is a mature marsh, characterized by many intricate branching tide creeks and pools which are separated by lush green vegetated banks. Cattails are the dominant plant. South Bay is shallow and more open. Bob describes it as "pre-marsh." He says that a few tide creeks, visible from the edge of the bay at low tide, are beginning to form, and eventually, as sedimentation builds up, South Bay will become more marsh-like.

The rushing waters of the Saw Kill tumble noisily into the bay just south of the Field Station; the forested shoreline curves around the mouth of the creek. To the west, the causeway of the railroad separates South Bay from the main river; silver Amtrak trains speeding across these tracks appear to be amphibious to an onlooker on the shore. A high wooded bluff rises up behind us, and mixed deciduous trees and evergreens seem to be slipping down the steep hillside almost into the bay. Farther to the west and north the Catskills form a hazy blue backdrop.

The outgoing tide has exposed a broad expanse of mud along the shore. These extensive mudflats are dotted with many thousands of bright emerald-green leaf rosettes. Each rosette consists of several glossy diamond-shaped leaves with toothed margins and measures seven to eleven inches across. Some are draped on rocks embedded in the mud; others embellish branches and logs which have been washed up by earlier tides. A little farther out, more rosettes float on the shallow water left by the ebbing tide. They are the only visible portion of an import- ed plant, the Eurasian water-chestnut, that has invaded the Hudson River and other waterways in the Northeast.

Wedged in among the water-chestnut rosettes are many curious tiny plants, each made up of a circular green "leaf" about a quarter of an inch wide floating

on the surface, with several threadlike rootlets hanging down in the water. These minute plants, one of our smallest flowering plants, are called duckweed because they are a favorite food of ducks. They often cover the surface of small ponds, marshes, and garden pools. Here, sheltered from the wind and currents, the duckweeds thrive among the water-chestnut rosettes.

As my gaze travels outward, I realize that a nearly solid green carpet covering the bay as far as I can see consists of countless more water-chestnut rosettes, almost obscuring the water. When I visited South Bay in early June only a few small rosettes appeared here and there. A few weeks later, they began to multiply rapidly, and now in less than a month the green mass blankets the bay.

To learn more about this prolific plant, I had asked Bob to accompany me today; he and other biologists have been conducting extensive research on water-chestnut and its effect on wildlife, especially the fishes, in places like Tivoli Bays.

Bob tells me that water-chestnut is an alien invader that has spread prolifically. With its handsome leaf rosettes, it was introduced as an ornamental in a pond in upstate New York in the late 1800s. It escaped into the Mohawk River in a flood and gradually spread down the Mohawk into the Hudson. By the 1950s, it had become widespread in

the Hudson River, as far south as Bear Mountain, where the water is slightly brackish. It is found in Connecticut, Massachusetts, and Vermont. In the mid-Hudson Valley it has also spread to some farm ponds and streams; Canada geese may carry the seeds in their plumage, or seeds might be dispersed in clothing or on vehicles.

The water-chestnut originated in Eurasia. In eastern Europe, Asia, and Africa, it has long been prized for its edible nut, high in protein. It is not related to the Chinese water-chestnut, which many of us have savored in Oriental dishes.

Under each floating leaf rosette in the bay are little stalks with inflated bladders which keep the rosette afloat. A long flexible stem with water roots and feathery rootlike leaves extends down into the water. As the plant matures, nuts, each containing one seed, develop and anchor themselves and the plant in the bottom mud. The nut, green at first and eventually black, is about three-quarters of an inch across and has four large barbed spikes. These spikes can inflict painful damage on bare feet or even pierce one's sneakers. In late fall and winter heaps of the blackened nut husks, washed up by the tides, can be seen along the shore of the river and the tidal coves. Thousands more remain buried in the bottom sediments long after the leaves and stems disintegrate in early September. Seeds can survive five years or

A researcher in South Bay checks her drift net.

longer in the sediment.

Why is water-chestnut considered detrimental? I ask. Bob explains that it chokes out plants such as native wild-celery and Eurasian watermilfoil, which are important wildlife food; waterfowl cannot eat water-chestnut. The dense leaf mats coat the water surface so sunlight can't get down to the bottom, preventing other rooted plants from growing. They also slow down currents that flow through, causing sediments to fall to the bottom, and speed the filling of ponds and bays.

The sharp spiny nuts are hazardous in swimming areas, and from late June to late September it is impossible to boat in areas infested with water-chestnut. The tough underwater stems can wrap around outboard motors and river buoys. I personally learned how it impedes a canoe when I went out into South Bay with researchers participating in the water-chestnut study. Three of us waded in. With difficulty, we pushed and pulled the loaded canoe through the thick mat of floating rosettes, while the tangle of underwater stems wrapped around our legs.

Many methods have been tried to control water-chestnut. The DEC tried to eradicate it in South Bay by applying a herbicide, 2,4-D, for fifteen years through 1976, but stopped spraying when the bad effects of pesticides became better known. Hand-pulling the weed has proved effective, but it has to be continued for five years or longer, and no seeds can be left to germinate. The Town of Esopus, on the west shore of the Hudson River, annually has a public water-chestnut-clearing event to improve the town swimming beach. Many volunteers participate in the hand-pulling. Mechanical harvesting is also effective, but prohibitively expensive.

On the positive side, research has shown that larval and juvenile fish of several species thrive in water-chestnut beds, which offer good shelter from predators and plentiful food organisms such as worms, crustaceans, insects, and spiders that inhabit the plants. Water-measurer bugs, damselfly adults, water-lily leaf beetles, marsh lady beetles, and other insects populate the leaves above water, and many kinds of larvae, snails, water-fleas, and other organisms live on the underwater parts. If you shake a water-chestnut plant over a white tray, you can examine some of this fascinating community of miniature creatures with a magnifying glass.

The researchers conducted comparative studies of fish found in water-chestnut beds with those frequenting native wild-celery and Eurasian watermilfoil in other parts of Tivoli Bays. They concluded that water-chestnut stands provide a significant nursery for Hudson River forage fishes, such as banded killifish, spottail shiners, juvenile carp, and goldfish. They also felt that eradication of water-chestnut in the Hudson might not be the best possible option even if it were biologically and economically feasible. Some solution might be found, they suggested, to thin out portions of the beds in the shallows, yet "maintain and improve the value of the water-chestnut beds to fish while reducing the problems for fishers and boaters."[1] Bob now thinks that water-chestnut is detrimental for some small native fish species. Research is continuing to find the answers.

R. Schmidt ©

Like the water-chestnut, many other northeastern plants and animals are immigrants. Some have been introduced deliberately for food, medicine, research, or beauty; some have arrived accidentally, hitch-hiking in ships' ballast or cargoes, even clinging to the bottom of ships, or entering the country in other devious ways.

"When human beings move organisms such as plants, birds, and fish around on the face of the earth, they may get out of control, and some non-native species spread and become detrimental, while others don't," Bob states.

Among other imported plants and animals which have become naturalized in the Hudson Valley and far beyond, Bob mentions purple loosestrife, common reed (there is a less-invasive native strain), yellow iris, mute swans, carp and goldfish, zebra mussels, Japanese beetles, and a host of others. When they immigrate from their native habitats, they may leave behind the natural predators or diseases which control them and can run riot in their adopted surroundings. Some are entirely benign; some crowd out native species; all of them, in the eyes of some ecologists, may threaten world-wide biodiversity. I am intrigued by the almost endless list of invasive plants and surprised to learn that familiar and lovely roadside flowers like day-lilies and Queen Anne's lace are also aliens.

A few days after my enlightening look at the water-chestnut, I walk along the western edge of North Bay, where it is bordered by the railway embankment, to photograph some purple loose-strife. Having long admired the attractive purple-red flowering spikes, I now want to examine them with a different eye.

The north end of the bay looks like a rolling green meadow, so thick is the growth of cattail and spatterdock. The tidal water is hidden by the lush growth. Bordering the bank is a colorful band of

Above: Myriad rosettes almost obscure the surface of South Bay in July.

Below: Each water-chestnut rosette is composed of several shiny leaves.

The lovely magenta flowers of purple loosestrife become a "purple peril" as this alien invades the wetlands.

flowers—great pink trumpets of bindweed, related to morning glory; four-petaled sunny yellow evening primroses; little orange and yellow pouches of a flower descriptively called butter and eggs or toadflax; leafy stalks of viper's bugloss, its small purple-blue blossoms with protruding red stamens arranged along the stem. Large clusters of white blooms decorate a ninebark shrub; some clusters exhibit variegated red and green fruits. The flowers on Bell's honeysuckle have already been replaced by numerous red berries, attractive to many birds, even though the shrub is another alien which crowds out native species.

Down on the bank at the edge of the bay is a large clump of purple loosestrife, almost shrub-like, with magenta flower spikes thrusting five to six feet above a jungle of woody stems. The solid mass of vivid color, set off by a nearby cluster of bright yellow coneflowers, is spectacular against the green of cattail leaves and the blue of the sky. Loosestrife's beauty is probably one of the factors that has aided its spread. Some nurseries stock loosestrife varieties, and gardeners plant them.

Although its exact origins are not known, loosestrife may have been brought here as a garden plant from the Old World, or its tiny seeds may have arrived accidentally in ship ballast. It appeared in the Hudson Valley about 1800. By the early part of the 1900s, loosestrife was becoming common and widespread. Now it is known from coast to coast in the United States and southern Canada. It is especially prolific in the Northeast. It flourishes in moist or wet soil, and its purple blooms can be found from June to September in roadside ditches, on the banks of streams and ponds, in marshes and other wetlands. It can also grow in dry soil in the absence of competition. Loosestrife is common in the Hudson River tidal wetlands as far south as the saline waters of

Piermont Marsh in Rockland County.[2]

This "purple peril," as it has been called, has many successful means of dispersal. Each flowering stalk produces some 300,000 seeds—twenty-four billion seeds per acre! The minute seeds are spread by wind, float on water, and ride to new destinations on animal fur, human clothing, and vehicles. Pieces of broken stalks can fall into the water and sprout. A clump of the woody base can slip off a bank as the soil erodes and be moved by water or ice to a spot where it takes root again.

As loosestrife continues to spread, biologists have become concerned that it is crowding out native wetland plants like cattails, sedges, and bulrushes, and feel that it is of little value to marsh wildlife. Muskrats and other marsh inhabitants feast on cattails and bulrushes, but eat little loosestrife.

Large cattail stands in the Northeast are critical nesting habitat for several marsh birds—the least bittern, king rail, common moorhen, and marsh wren—and important, but not sole, nesting habitat for American bittern, northern harrier, Virginia rail, and sora. A few of these birds nest in mixed cattail-loosestrife stands, but almost never in loosestrife.

On the other hand, red-winged blackbirds prefer loosestrife for nesting, and American goldfinches frequently nest in this bushy plant. Deer graze on it, and many insects, which might provide sustenance for marsh birds, feed on it.[3]

Its negative attributes, however, outweigh its advantages, and many methods of control and eradication have been tried. "You can burn it . . . you can spray it . . . you can flood it . . . you can mow it . . . you can beat it with a stick . . . but this persistent pest is harder to kill than Godzilla, and nearly as destructive," an environmental magazine states.[4]

Scientists are now experimenting with some voracious loosestrife-eating beetles, imported from Europe where the plant probably originated. They feast exclusively on purple loosestrife, so should not cause other problems. Cornell University is mass-producing the leaf-eating beetles and recently set free several thousand of the creatures in the Montezuma National Wildlife Refuge near Seneca Falls. The noxious purple weed has invaded over 1500 acres of wetlands in the refuge, choking out native plants and threatening the waterfowl and other animals which need them for survival. Biologists say it may take several years for the beetles to control the loosestrife, but they are hoping it will work.

Farther south along the edge of the marsh, I come across still another plant which is invading Tivoli North Bay: common reed, often referred to by its scientific name, *Phragmites*. A member of the grass family, the bamboo-like reed is known in various

Using common reed and purple loosestrife to camouflage a duck hunter's blind helps spread these invasive plants in the bays.

parts of the country by many other names, among them giant reed, cane, mare's tail, foxtail, roseau, carrizo cane, and quill reed. Growing about twenty-five feet offshore in the tidal shallows is a dense stand of these very tall thin reeds, ten to fourteen feet high, taller even than the cattails. Each stem is topped by a soft feathery plume waving gently in the breeze. In the early summer the new plumes are purplish. In the fall they turn pale and straw-colored. The tough, slow-to-decay, tasseled stalks stand almost intact throughout the winter. The smaller plumed stems of this attractive plant are often used in dried flower arrangements.

There is debate as to whether common reed is native or introduced or both. Archeological findings indicate that it was present in this country thousands of years ago. One interesting archeological discovery, unearthed at the Red Bow cliff dwellings in Arizona, consisted of several hundred prehistoric "cigarettes." The cigarette barrels were made from stems of the reed and stuffed with tobacco. When the cigarettes were smoked, the tobacco burned, but the tough reed stems did not, and they were used again.[5]

On travels around the country, I have observed common reed in roadside ditches, in vacant lots, on the edges of marshes, swamps, and construction sites, as far south as Florida and Texas, west to California, across Canada to British Columbia. Throughout the mid-Hudson Valley, its tall plumes wave at the edges of shopping centers and along highway shoulders and medians, especially in moist disturbed places, as well as in the tidal coves, fresh and brackish, along the river.

Canoeing in Tivoli North Bay, I have found places where this "weed" has taken hold. It may start where a duck blind has been built or repaired, and the soil around it disturbed. Hunters may camouflage a blind with reeds, parts of which may break off and

take root. Once established, the reed spreads from horizontal runners either underground or aboveground. These runners can grow prodigiously, like Jack's beanstalk. Along the edge of one large tide creek in North Bay there is an immense wall of reeds. Cattails have not penetrated this stand, although some lesser vegetation such as jewelweed and arrow arum grow in the reed bed.

Common reed seems to be of less value to wildlife than native plants like cattail that it replaces. The leaves are too tough to be eaten by most wildlife. It is not without some value however. A few animals like muskrats eat it, and use it for lodge building. Black-capped chickadees forage for insects in common reed, and some birds nest in it. The dense stands may also provide important cover for wildlife.

Burning, mechanical harvesting, spraying of herbicides, repeated mowing, and other methods have been used in some areas to control the spread of common reed. It may be a threat in some wetlands, but harmless or beneficial in others. Although unwelcome in most parts of this country, in other countries reed has many uses: thatch, food, fuel, paper, feed for domestic animals, nets, shafts for fishing spears. It is also used for weaving, fencing, and building. It might be possible to develop similar uses for reed materials here. Harvesting for such uses would help to control it.

As I photograph the offshore stand of reeds, my attention is diverted by the loud swishing of wings over the river behind me. Turning around I watch a pair of graceful white swans land in the river and glide effortlessly a short distance downstream, where they begin to feed on some underwater vegetation. These majestic birds are mute swans. Like the loosestrife and water-chestnut, they are immigrants to our shores. Although beloved by many for their grace and beauty and celebrated throughout the ages in song and legend, the handsome birds are cause for concern among many wildlife biologists. They feel that the rapidly multiplying numbers of this non-native swan are a threat to native waterfowl. Mute swans uproot and sometimes deplete aquatic plants as they graze ceaselessly for food in shallow ponds by day and on moonlight nights. In some areas they harass and attack the native ducks and geese that invade their nesting areas. Some swans, accustomed to being fed by admiring humans, may even attack people when no food is available. Reports from several states indicate that mute swan populations are experiencing unrestricted growth, increasing by thirty to forty percent each year.

The mute swan, native to Europe and Asia, adapts readily to other environments, and today it occurs in many parts of the world. Swan fossils from the Pleistocene Age have been found in Ireland, England, Germany, Denmark, Portugal, Italy, and Azerbaijan. This elegant bird is a recurring figure in mythology and folklore, painting, music, and poetry. Some of Tchaikovsky's most beautiful music was written for his famous ballet, "Swan Lake," the story of the beautiful Princess Odette, who has been cast under a spell by a wicked magician and turned into a swan. The spell can only be broken if she finds a man who swears to love no one but her. Through many trials, the love of Siegfried and Odette finally triumphs, and the spell is broken. The dances reveal the swans moving in graceful patterns and transfer some of the elegance and beauty of the birds to the stage.

In England, where the swan was semi-domesti-

A wall of common reed tops a tide bank in North Bay.

cated as early as the twelfth century, the beloved birds live in great numbers in close association with humans. The ponds in London's parks have hundreds of swans, as do the great manor houses throughout England. The crown claims partial ownership of the birds. Because the swans are royal birds, possessing them is considered a mark of prestige and distinction in England.

In this country the birds apparently were first imported to grace large eastern estates. A group of mute swans was introduced in 1910 in the mid-Hudson Valley near Rhinebeck and in 1912 on Long Island at Southampton and Oakdale, according to New York bird expert John Bull.[6] Escaped birds

A long line of mute swans swims across South Bay in almost military precision.

readily reproduced in the wild, and today mute swans are abundant along the Atlantic Flyway. They nest in shallow ponds and marshes, usually along the coast. Chesapeake Bay has a large population of breeding swans. They are especially numerous in the bays and ponds of eastern Long Island. Populations are reported from Rhode Island, Connecticut, Massachusetts, New Jersey, Ohio, and Pennsylvania. In Traverse Bay, Michigan, a single escaped pair grew to a flock of 1000 swans in three decades.

Swans can be seen in Tivoli Bays and the adjoining Hudson River until a deep winter freeze sets in. Then they gather by the hundreds in larger lakes and bays downriver where the water does not freeze, or where they can keep it open by the movement of their bodies and wings. By spring they have dispersed up and down the river or returned to the ponds and marshes where they nest.

In addition to the introduced mute swan, there are two native swans in North America—the tundra swan, which breeds in the far north and winters on the seacoasts of the United States, and the trumpeter swan of the Northwest. The mute swan is easily distinguished from the others by its graceful curved neck and its bright orange bill. The native swans have straight "broomstick" necks and black bills. The mute swan, with a wing span of seven to eight feet, is not only the heaviest of the three species, but the heaviest of our flying birds, usually weighing from twenty to twenty-six pounds, with some individuals weighing up to fifty pounds.

Although called "mute," the swan does have a voice. It hisses, grunts, and makes snoring sounds. Wild swans, especially in the spring, have a call that carries a long distance. The young, called cygnets, peep like baby chicks or ducklings. About half of the mute swan population lives to age seven, while a few, mostly females, have been known to live to age fifty. The male is called the cob and the female the pen. They usually mate by age two or three, and once they

select a mate, they remain bonded for life, a trait which further endears this bird to humans.

No swan nests have been found in Tivoli Bays, although the birds frequent our area, sometimes in great numbers. I once witnessed a "herd" of about fifty swans, swimming in military precision in a long line in South Bay. Swans nest farther south along the river. The nests, built by both the male and female, are large structures, heaped high with reeds, sticks, and grass. They may be used for several years.

A number of methods are being tried to control the rapid population growth of the mute swans, despite the opposition of many members of the general public. In Rhode Island, biologists from the state Division of Fish and Wildlife have attempted to control the swans' spread by a controversial procedure known as shaking the eggs. After locating nests by helicopter, they visit the nests by boat and methodically shake each egg in the nests, scrambling the yolks to prevent hatching. After the eggs are replaced in the nests, the unsuspecting swans continue to incubate them until it is too late in the season to lay a second clutch. Swan-loving humans protest; school children write hate letters; the biologists are called killers. Swans have been admired and revered for centuries, and it is difficult to convince most people that they constitute a menace.

I find it interesting that many of the alien invaders which have infiltrated the wetlands also add beauty and interest to our native flora and fauna. It is important to study these introduced species but not to feel that drastic control methods always need to be taken. Species that may pose threats to native vegetation and wildlife in some places may be harmless or beneficial in other tidal or non-tidal habitats, or have positive aspects wherever they appear. Some biologists may feel that they threaten biodiversity, but, in a way, many of these alien species also add diversity.

A spectacular dragonfly with iridescent wings pauses on a grass stem.

5 AUGUST

Mummichogs, Monsters, and Dragons of the Air

August is the culmination of summer in the wetlands. Colors are everywhere. Many-hued flowers bloom alongside the trails, around the wet edges of the bays, and in huge mats on the water–pale pink of swamp rose, rosy-pink of bindweed, burnt orange and yellow of jewelweed, fire-engine red of cardinal flower, violet of pickerelweed, lavender of aster, magenta of loosestrife, pale yellow of evening-primrose, pumpkin yellow of spatterdock, delicate white of arrowhead, rich brown of cattail spikes. The herbacious vegetation on and under the water is many shades of green–midnight green, slate green, chartreuse, olive, muddy green, even some brownish greens.

Although the autumn equinox is still several weeks away, I feel stirrings of fall in Tivoli Bays in August. Plants and animals are beginning to prepare for winter: plants are setting seed; some animals are storing food in their body fat; some, like the squirrels and chipmunks, are gathering fruits and nuts and hiding them in secret places. Contrarily, snapping turtles stop eating toward the middle of the month, preparing for the long winter in the bottom mud.

Blackbirds gather in flocks and leave the marsh by day to feast in nearby grain fields before migration.

By August's end a few red leaves begin to appear on the red maples, the woodbine, and the poison-ivy vine. While the "dog days" of summer are still with us, fall signals that it is near.

August is glorious at its peak, a perfect time to spend hours canoeing in North Bay. At mid-month, I am paddling languidly with a friend through this watery paradise to observe high summer at low tide. Great rafts of spatterdock fill the smaller channels and make them impassable. The spatterdock leaves have lost their spring luster and are dull, muddy, and pitted with insect holes. Down among the leaves the golden globes of the flowers still shine out like lighted lanterns. A few will bloom into October.

Weaving our way around the spatterdock, we are confronted by a vast violet-blue "meadow," extending over several acres. The "meadow" is made up of countless spires of pickerelweed, an emergent plant rising two to four feet out of the shallow water. It has large arrowhead-shaped leaves; the flowers are clustered in showy three-inch terminal spikes that

A violet-blue spire of pickerelweed emerges from the shallows.

resemble hyacinths. We guide the bow of the canoe in among the pickerelweeds to anchor it in the thick growth. Our eyes are filled with the violet beauty of the flower spikes, backlighted by the afternoon sun, and our ears are filled with the sound of a million whirring, buzzing, flying insects which have come to feast on the nectar of the flowers or on each other. There are honey bees and wasps, beetles and butterflies, ladybugs and hover flies, moths and midges. They are all sizes, shapes, and colors. Winged and wingless, fat and thin, round and elongated, and every color of the spectrum.

Some insects are crawling on the stems; some are poking into the tubular flowers on the spires. The stamens of each pickerelweed flower are so situated that when an insect enters the bloom to sip its nectar, it brushes against the pollen-loaded anther (the head of the stamen), and soon transfers some of the fairy

Water-lily leaf beetle

dust clinging to its body to another flower, aiding in pollination.

Lurking above the flowering spikes are giant dragons of the air, the dragonflies, and their smaller slimmer relatives, the damselflies. Easily distinguished from each other, dragonflies rest with their wings stiffly outspread, while most damselflies fold their wings over their backs when they alight. Dragonflies have been called devil's darning needles, and it was once said they could sew up the lips of wicked people or naughty children. They have also been called snake doctors, mule killers, mosquito hawks, and gauze flies. The names make them sound dangerous, and so they are–but never to humans; they prey only on other insects. They are extremely beneficial, consuming numerous mosquitoes and other harmful insects.

Dragonflies are also among our most beautiful insects, with their large gauzy many-veined wings and long slim bodies, some measuring up to three-and-a-half inches. Many are brightly colored, glowing in green and gold, spotted or banded in orange, red, cobalt, black, cinnamon brown, violet, even purple, while the slender damselflies glitter in metallic blue and green. Alfred Tennyson called dragonflies "living flashes of light." Their common names are descriptive: amberwing, blue and green darner, clubtail, green-eyed skimmer, blue pirate, jagged-edge saddleback, twelve spot, bluet, among others. There are about 400 species of dragonflies and damselflies in America, and almost 5000 worldwide.

Identifying dragonflies is difficult for me. In Tivoli Bays I have seen brown dragonflies with black spots on their wings. A very large pale blue creature hovered over the canoe at the

Stony Creek Landing recently. Once a gorgeous dragonfly with a bright red body alighted on the back of my companion, but didn't stay long enough to be photographed. Most of the damselflies I have noted in Tivoli Bays are bluets, named for their iridescent blue bodies.

Like snapping turtles and other creatures, dragonflies date back to prehistoric times. Their ancestors, with a wingspread of almost thirty inches, were the largest insects that ever lived. They soared over the primitive swamps of the Carboniferous Age 200,000,000 years ago. Their fossilized remains have been found in Colorado, Kansas, Siberia, and other parts of the world. They have been the subject of painting and poetry throughout the centuries. Their images may be found on ancient pottery; Oriental scrolls; medieval manuscripts, paintings, and jewelry; and other art forms.

These breathtakingly beautiful creatures are ferocious predators. Making a basket out of their front legs, they catch and devour their prey on the wing. The dragonflies' hunting is aided by their remarkable compound eyes, which may have as many as 25,000 lenses, enabling them to look up

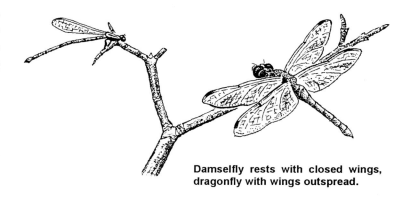

Damselfly rests with closed wings, dragonfly with wings outspread.

Morning clouds fill the sky over spatterdock in Tivoli North Bay.

and down and from side to side. Their flight is extremely efficient and speedy. They can fly up to thirty-five miles an hour, brake and stop instantly, fly backward, hover, turn swiftly.

Dragonflies also mate on the wing. Witnessing this phenomenon is an unforgettable experience. Once I watched with fascination as a flying dragon caught another dragonfly, most certainly a female, by locking its legs around her. The male then curved his abdomen around and fastened it to the back of her head. Thus coupled, they flew off out of my sight. While mating they might fly in tandem for up to an hour. While they are in flight, the male transfers his sperm to the female. Egg laying soon takes place, the female dipping low over the water, sometimes with the male still attached, as she deposits her eggs.

The eggs hatch in the water into ugly brown or green creatures called nymphs, which breathe through gills and are even more ferocious predators than the winged adults they later become. They lie in wait in the mud or among the submerged pond weeds. When another insect larva or water bug swims by, the nymph shoots out a long hinged underlip, which unfolds into a treacherous appendage with pincers at the tip. Grabbing its victim, the dragonfly nymph folds its lip back again, pulling its hapless prey into its wide mouth, where it is promptly devoured. The nymphs may take a year or longer to develop, and as they get older, they even catch tadpoles and small fish. In turn they may be eaten by larger fish, becoming part of the food chain in the marsh.

As it grows, the nymph goes through

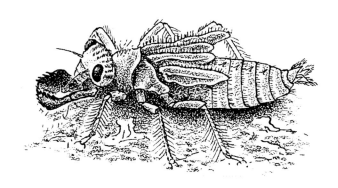

Dragonfly nymph[1]

several molts under water, discarding its skin each time. Finally, when it is ready to become an adult, it climbs out of the water onto a plant stem. There its hard outer skin splits open, and the adult crawls out. As its damp wings unfold, the dragonfly pumps blood into the vast network of veins, and it soon flies off into the sunshine. The ugly nymph has been transformed into a spectacular airborne dragonfly. The empty translucent shell of its former self remains intact, still attached to the plant stem like a ghostly creature.

⊛ ⊛ ⊛

One August day several years ago, when I was first starting my marsh explorations, I was privileged to attend an all-day canoe seminar on Tivoli North Bay, conducted by my son, Erik. I remember that day as an exciting hands-on learning experience in the ecology of a fresh-water tidal marsh, as he introduced us to the wonders of the wetland: plants and fish, birds and bugs, and all manner of organisms on and in the water. I was especially intrigued by Erik's description of the abundant fish, many with odd names like alewives and mummichogs, that inhabit the marsh and the river.

Our little flotilla of canoes embarked from the Stony Creek landing into North Bay, where the incredible abundance of life in the tidal waters was immediately apparent. Noisy splashes marked the presence of large fish jumping out of the water. Erik identified them as common carp, an alien fish. In Tivoli Bays they average about ten pounds in weight. A record carp, caught in North Bay by fish scientist Bob Schmidt, weighed twenty-four pounds and was thirty-two inches long. Several years ago when I was canoeing on North Bay a tremendous carp suddenly arched up out of the water no more than two feet away. It was a startling and frightening experience. If the monstrous fish had been any closer it might have swamped the fragile craft. This specimen must have been about three feet long! To my inexperienced eyes it looked like the Loch Ness monster.

Carp are native to Europe and Asia and now occur throughout New York State and most of this continent. They spawn in Tivoli Bays from late spring to August, each female laying thousands of eggs. C. Lavett Smith, formerly of the American Museum of Natural History, reported that a fifteen-and-a-half inch female had 36,000 eggs and a thirty-three-and-a-half-inch fish contained 2,208,000 eggs.[2]

One very warm day in mid-June this past year I witnessed the frenzied spawning activity of carp in Tivoli South Bay, where an unusual amount of splashing and movement had attracted me to the edge of the water. It was low tide; only about a foot of water remained near the shore. Dozens of huge speckled fish were thrashing about in the shallows and swimming crazily back and forth in their courtship maneuvers. Several feet farther out other monstrous

fish were jumping out of the water and coming down with great splashes. The carp ranged in size from about one-and-a-half to two-and-a-half feet in length. Sometimes two swam side by side; sometimes they swam head to tail. At other times, four or five swam in a group, their backs protruding out of the shallow water. Presumably at least one fish in each group was a female, pursued by several ardent males.

As we paddled slowly around North Bay, hundreds of miniature fish skipped unceasingly in silver showers around our boats. Their tiny splashes created a rhythmic orchestral beat while they danced in and out of the water in a ballet-like sequence. One landed in my canoe; it was about two inches long.

Canoeists paddle around North Bay.

"They're mummichogs," Erik said. "They skip out of the water when they are disturbed." This oddly-named little fish was called "mummichoa" by Algonquian-speaking Native Americans, and the name gradually became mummichog. It is a species of killifish, an important link in the food chain in the marsh.

Two volunteers were asked to take a seine net into the shallow water. When they pulled up the dripping net, they had caught a pumpkinseed, a kind of sunfish; several killifish; and two young herring—an alewife and a shad. About forty species of fish have been caught in South and North Bay, while outside in the river, fishermen catch white catfish, American shad, and striped bass. Spottail shiners, sunfish and

A young girl cleans a white perch caught in North Bay.

bluegills, killifish, and tesselated darters spawn in the bays, and striped bass and two species of herring—American shad and blueback herring—spawn in the deeper Hudson. The alewives also spawn in the marsh and in Stony Creek, wherever there are rocks, according to Erik.

One of the most common fish caught in Tivoli Bays is the white perch, which seems most plentiful near the railroad embankment. Goldfish, an introduced species, related to carp, are also found in the bays and in the river. The goldfish in the river, unlike the three- or four-inch aquarium specimens familiar to most children, may grow to a length of twelve to fourteen inches. The Hudson River goldfish are usually olive in color; a few are bright orange or orange-red.

The goldfish, a native of eastern Asia, was widely introduced into North America before 1832. It can be found almost anywhere in New York State, according to Smith.[3] Goldfish once flourished and reproduced in the Hudson, but they are now scarce. In any event, if someone tells you a tale of catching a monster goldfish in Tivoli Bays, it's not just another fish story!

The most fascinating fish which Erik described for us is the eel. Our only catadromous fish, it lives as a juvenile in fresh water like Tivoli Bays, and when it becomes an adult, travels down an estuary such as the Hudson River to the Atlantic Ocean to spawn in salt water. Its spawning grounds are probably in the Sargasso Sea near Bermuda. After hatching, the tiny, transparent larval fish miraculously make their way to the coast where they transform into miniature eels known as elvers. The elvers swim up estuaries until they reach fresh water areas. Elvers are abundant in Tivoli Bays, as well as in many other creeks and lakes far from the ocean.

The young eels are snake-like in shape, long and

thin, at first gray-green in color, becoming yellow-brown as they grow. After several years they become silver as they mature and move out to sea. In Tivoli Bays elvers feed on insects such as mayflies and caddisflies, and on crustaceans.

In the 1950s, a few years after my husband and I established our children's camp, youngsters fishing from the dock in the pond occasionally caught wriggling eels. As far as I can remember, the eels were a foot or two long. At the time, ignorant of such unusual creatures as catadromous fish, I wondered how eels from the ocean mysteriously arrived in our pond, which was about five miles east of the Hudson River and ninety miles north of the sea. Now, almost fifty years later, I learn that these strange fish are experts at making their way upstream over dams and rocks and small waterfalls, and occasionally even travel overland, probably on rainy nights.

As we talked about eels, Erik dipped his hand into the water and pulled up several strands of a very thin ribbonlike leaf about a yard long. "This is wild-celery," he said. "It's one of several species of submerged, or sub-tidal, aquatic plants which flourish in North Bay. The little tubers developing on it are good duck food." He showed us other underwater plants that are valuable as food or shelter or both for animals. Most aquatic plants support a multitude of tiny larvae, worms, and snails, which feed on their leaves, and in turn are good food for fish. Among these plants are Eurasian watermilfoil, an introduced species, also tall and thin, but with many small leaves (milfoil means "thousand leaves"); coontail, a plant with tiny narrow leaves in bushy whorls that give it its name; clasping

pondweed; and waterweed or elodea.

We also observed plants like water-chestnut and duckweeds with leaves floating on the surface of the water and true emergent plants, growing upright out of shallow water near shore and on the banks bordering the tide channels. Erik picked specimens of four emergent plants which all have heart- or arrow-shaped leaves: spatterdock, pickerelweed, arrow arum, and arrowhead. Under his tutelage, we began to learn how to tell them apart.

Spatterdock has a large broad fleshy heart-shaped leaf, over a foot long and almost as wide, with a very heavy midrib underneath. The plants bear single globular yellow flowers, standing upright on thick stems and almost hidden by the leaves.

Pickerelweed has an elongated narrow heart-shaped leaf, a foot or more in length, on a long stem; it is very heart-like at the bottom with shallow rounded lobes. Its numerous violet-blue flowers are borne in tall upright spikes as described earlier.

Two volunteers drag a seine net through shallow water.

Spatterdock

Arrowhead leaves

Broad-leaved arrowhead and arrow arum have arrow-shaped leaves similar to each other, difficult for an amateur wetland observer to tell apart. The leaf of arrowhead, especially on the specimens in North Bay, is usually obtuse (somewhat blunt) at the tip of the leaf. All the veins radiate from the tip of the leaf stalk. From July to September, arrowhead displays delicate white three-petaled flowers with yellow centers. The blooms are about an inch wide. The fruits are little green balls in clusters.

The leaf of arrow arum has a tiny spine at the tip; the secondary veins are arranged along a mid-rib, and do not reach the edge of the leaf. The flowers are inconspicuous.

While we puzzled over the differences among this quartet of common wetland plants, Erik offered an explanation of why so many marsh plants have similar shapes. "There are two shapes common to many emergent plants which grow in shallow water or around the wet edges of swamps and marshes.

They are sword-shaped like the leaves of cattail and sweet flag, or heart- and arrow-shaped. The shape has something to do with their staying above the surface of the water and not being torn apart by currents."

As he led us down a wide tide channel, a line of ripples revealed a small creature, a muskrat, swimming toward the bank, only its dark brown head visible. At our approach, it dived under and disappeared. We waited quietly but it did not surface again. The muskrat is one of the more visible mammals that live in the tidal marsh. An adult muskrat is about twenty inches long, including its long black nearly naked tail, which is almost half of that length. The distinctive tail is flattened from side to side. This little denizen of the marsh has rich brown shiny fur, prized by trappers.

Over-trapping in the past may have contributed to the severe decline of muskrats in Hudson River marshes. The muskrat population in Tivoli Bays crashed in the mid-1970s. Causes for the decline vary

Arrowhead fruit and flowers

Arrow arum

in different marshes. Toxic substances, disease, raccoon predation, and vegetation change could be other contributing factors.[4]

While we watched for the elusive muskrat, Erik suggested that it may have dived into an underwater entrance of a burrow in the muddy bank. Muskrats live in burrows where there are banks with cohesive soil, like those in tidal North Bay. The burrow may extend for many feet, with other underwater entrances and with nest chambers in the bank above the high water level.

Muskrats also build bulky conical lodges of marsh vegetation in shallow water. The structure has underwater entrances; the peak rises above the surface of the water. Some lodges may be found in North Bay, but the local muskrats seem to prefer bank burrows for feeding, nesting, and raising their young. The burrows and lodges also provide valuable shelter and nesting areas for many other creatures such as small fish in the watery doorways, turtles,

waterfowl, and rodents. On hot days I have frequently seen large snapping turtles, head in, resting in the entrances, only the tips of their tails visible.

The pond at our children's camp had a large muskrat house near the far shore, which was utilized for several years, and we had many opportunities to watch the engaging muskrats which swam, frolicked, and raised their families in the pond. I recall a fascinating experience once when I was ice skating on the first clear freeze in late fall. As I skimmed over the pond, I spotted a muskrat swimming under the ice and followed it for several minutes as it zig-zagged speedily around. I eventually lost sight of the little pond dweller when it neared its lodge, and a mass of vegetation in the shallows obscured my view through the ice. How I wished I could have shrunk in size and been able to follow the furry creature into its den, like Alice in Wonderland magically pursuing the White Rabbit down its hole!

Following our muskrat sighting in North Bay,

Erik commented that only a few other mammals enter the open tidal marsh. "These include mink, Norway rat, an occasional raccoon or opossum, some deer. Reptiles and amphibians are also not well represented in the Hudson's fresh water tidal marshes. They can't stand the fluctuating water levels."

I am aware of at least one beaver in North Bay; it seems to reside somewhere near the northernmost bridge in the railway embankment. A fisherman once told me he frequently saw it at the bridge. Over the years, I have spotted the beaver there a few times. One spring afternoon, canoeing with education coordinator Dennis Mildner and a class of high school students, a large beaver slipped off a bank. The brown furry mammal swam unafraid near our group of excited young people, acting as though Dennis had invited it to perform!

As we reached the railroad causeway, Erik pointed out that the embankment, built on fill in 1850, is responsible for a large portion of marsh development along the Hudson. It cuts off the bays from the main channel of the river. The silt and other suspended materials settle out as the tides come into the marsh and the current slows, and the deposits accumulate over the years. North

Bay would have been a shallow open bay if not for the railroad. Among negative impacts of the railroad are diesel and noise pollution and herbicides, which may affect the marsh vegetation and wildlife in subtle ways.

⊛ ⊛ ⊛

One idyllic day toward August's end, I am enjoying a late afternoon paddle on North Bay with friends Denise and Richard. The canoe seems almost part of the marsh as it slips silently through the tide creeks, filled with mats of submerged water weeds and bordered by walls of waving cattails and loosestrife, with here and there a patch of golden yellow sunflower-like blooms called sneezeweed.

Our slim craft easily skirts along the edges of masses of pickerelweed, spatterdock, rushes, and arrowhead. Redwings flash their epaulets and chatter incessantly, flying back and forth in sociable little groups of eight or ten males, instead of shouting angrily at each other as they did in spring when they were defending their territories. Meadow grasshoppers are singing in a pulsating chorus from the greenery on the tide creek banks. Graceful tree swallows dip and skim over the surface of the water as they forage for insects, while stubby-tailed, short-necked kingfishers dive swiftly down, also feeding.

Pickerelweed in bloom draws a blue line across a tide channel.

Ripples mark the path of a patrolling muskrat, and the round dark head of a snapping turtle quickly disappears in a small circle of bubbles just ahead of us. Around a bend, a great blue heron fishing in a little cove, startled by our approach, flies up awkwardly and flaps away on great wings, its legs streaming stiffly out behind it, its neck in an S-curve. We may have disturbed his best catch of the day.

A marsh hawk takes wing as our canoe approaches.

An immature marsh hawk comes winging low over the cattails alongside the channel, also seeking its supper. The late afternoon sun shines on the rich russet of its belly and the white patch on its rump, as the young raptor glides and dips buoyantly on slender striated wings. That evening, looking up "marsh hawk" in my bird guide, I learn that marsh hawks are now known as "northern harriers." Intent on its hunting, the hawk seems unaware of our presence. We follow it, Richard paddling skillfully and silently, remaining about thirty yards behind the hawk. The graceful predator finally comes to rest on a rusty piece of fencing tilted up out of the marsh, striking a handsome pose for my camera. Although my zoom lens is extended to its full length of 210mm, it is not long enough to get a close-up shot. With just six frames left on the film, I carefully snap five of them, one at a time, as Richard maneuvers the canoe closer and closer, saving the last frame for that inevitable moment when the marsh hawk will take flight. When we are about twenty-five feet away, it suddenly turns and takes off, but its swift movement, combined with the slow motion of the canoe, slightly blurs the resulting photograph. Landscapes are much easier to photograph than birds; they don't move! The best shot of that incredibly beautiful hawk is the one that remains forever in my memory.

About seven o'clock, as the sun begins to sink lower, we start back toward the canoe landing, making our way along the eastern edge of the bay. The rays of the slowly descending sun cast a radiant glow across the marsh and light up a spectacular flash of intense scarlet cardinal flowers on the shore. These brilliant flowers are somewhat rare in our region, but they are blooming freely around the wet edges of North Bay this special August. With the canoe wedged firmly in the shoreline vegetation, I spend the next half hour photographing the tall scarlet spikes and am doubly rewarded when an exquisite black swallow-tail butterfly lights on a flower directly in front of my lens.

The sun has set in a blaze of color, and it is almost dark when we reach the dock. We carry the canoe and our gear up the steep bluff, and hoist the boat onto the car-top rack, tired but exhilarated by our paddle through the August marsh teeming with color, sound, and movement.

Early morning mist rises over Tivoli North Bay.

6 SEPTEMBER

Where the Closed Gentian Blooms

The canoe slips silently into the Stony Creek channel early one golden September morning. Gossamer strands of mist hover over the wetlands as the sun's first rays touch the cool surface of the water. Paddling slowly we see the marsh, in Thoreau's words, "throwing off its nightly clothing of mist, and here and there, by degrees, its soft ripples . . . were revealed, while the mists, like ghosts, were stealthily withdrawing in every direction . . ."[1]

Guiding the canoe around a bend in the channel, we catch a quick glimpse of a common yellowthroat, the sun glinting off its golden breast. The yellowthroat, a swamp-loving warbler, quickly disappears in a nearby thicket and scolds us with a repeated call that sounds like a sneeze, while a friendly chickadee, perched on the tip of a cattail, welcomes us with its familiar "chickadee-dee-dee."

Along the shore little water droplets are suspended from the delicate curving blades of grasses, a tiny twinkling sun reflected in each perfect globular drop. The thousand little suns are part of the magic of this early morning paddle on the marsh.

Some pale yellow leaves float past the canoe, their shadowy shapes twisting in the tide, which is moving rapidly outward to the river. The water is already very low; the smaller creeks and coves, choked with thick vegetation, are inaccessible. A companion paddling with me this morning guides the canoe into the main east-west passageway across the marsh. The broad, normally deep channel has taken on a different appearance in the low tide. Long thin strands of wild-celery float on the surface of the water like mermaid's hair, moving sinuously in the ebbing tide, while their stems remain anchored in the mud. A jungle of other underwater weeds is clearly visible in the shallow water.

The receding tide has exposed wide bands of mud on the cattail-arrow arum banks bordering the channel. In the sticky muck we can see the doorways of numerous muskrat burrows which were under water at high tide. Some burrows are disintegrating, crumbling from the constant battering of the tides; others are still intact.

Although August, with its riotous blooms and teeming wildlife, was the culmination of summer in the wetlands, this first week of September still

Small tubular flowers fan out from the perfect globe of a buttonbush bloom.

exhibits remnants of summer's abundance. A multitude of violet-blue spikes of pickerelweed stands erect in the shallows; the great mass of bloom is barely beginning to wane. Large clumps of purple loosestrife continue to flower uninhibited among the cattails. The deep purple patches are interspersed with small stands of late-blooming daisy-like flowers–sneezeweed and bur-marigold. Pale pink heads of Joe-Pye-weed, on seven-foot stems, are almost as high as the cattails and reeds.

A buttonbush shrub on the water's edge displays a few perfect globes covered with tubular white flowers, while some balls are already bearing nutlets.

Despite the promising sunrise, low clouds soon begin to gather, and the mountains on the horizon turn dark and somber. I hurriedly put my photo gear under cover as a few drops of rain trickle down. The scattered beads of rain become a gentle drizzle, and then a steady shower. The marsh appears even more beautiful in the rain.

The rain does not seem threatening, but concerned about my equipment, we reluctantly turn back. Just as we lift our canoe out of the water, the rain stops. A blue dragonfly with great filmy wings comes out of the vegetation and flies over the marsh, and the sun breaks through the clouds.

A week later, a beautiful sunny morning draws us out again. The sky is azure blue, mottled with gray and white cumulus clouds. The tide is flooding in the bay, as we launch our canoe. Although fall usually comes gradually to the wetlands, there is a marked change from last week. Two days of heavy rains in mid-week may have hastened the changes. The leaves of the red-osier dogwood shrubs fringing the shore have turned a deep wine-red color. Little bunches of white berries hang on blood-red stems among the leaves.

The flowers of the pickerelweed have almost disappeared. Purple loosestrife, however, is still blooming profusely, and fat fuzzy bees and other insects crawl over the flower spikes. Two dragonflies also hover over the loosestrife, waiting to pounce on unsuspecting insects.

Red and black butterflies flutter at intervals above the plants on the bank. A sharp-eyed osprey flies overhead, watching for fish in the fecund marsh waters. Several dark-colored ducks burst out of the water farther down the channel. Many creatures are hastening to get their fill of fish, berries, nectar, floating plants, or other abundant food, as they prepare for the advent of fall.

⊛　⊛　⊛

On a foggy, chilly twenty-first of the month, I visit North Bay to greet the fall equinox. Morning fogs occur frequently in the wetlands at this time of year. From the viewing platform overlooking the bay at the parking lot off Cruger Island Road, the lingering fog temporarily shuts out the distant view. In this

gray and silent world, only the marsh exists. The water is barely lapping against the shore. There is not a whisper of wind. The birds are silent. The cattails in the big pool in front of the overlook are dim and shadowy; the Catskills are invisible. In the eerie half-light I somehow feel closer to the essence of the marsh—its stillness, its wildness, its peacefulness.

My reflective mood is broken as a train rumbles across the railroad causeway. Chilled by the damp air, I decide to wait in the car until the fog lifts. When the sun begins to break through the fog, I gather up my camera and tripod and walk toward the viewing platform again.

In the growing light, my eye is drawn to a deep blue flower alongside the path. The exquisite bloom is an unusual shade of blue, the more striking now that many other flowers have faded. Although the roadsides and trail edges still display vivid purple asters, the incredible sky-blue color of this late-blooming flower surpasses the beauty of the asters. The plant is over a foot high. At the tip of the stem is a cluster of several upright tube-like flowers, each about two inches long. The petals are closed at the top with just a suggestion of a whitish fringe showing. The petals will remain closed; this unforgettable flower is a closed gentian. It is rare in the Hudson Valley, and this single specimen is the only time I have encountered it in the Research Reserve. Its cousin is the rare fringed gentian.

Three weeks later, in mid-October, I stop by the platform. Only one faded gentian blossom remains. The stunning sky-blue flowers have been transformed into a cluster of papery brown tube-like seed capsules. The brief glory of the closed gentian has disappeared until another season. Then perchance a tiny fragile seed from the dry capsule, wafted to another setting by the wind, may germinate and develop into a deep-blue beauty in early fall.

The overlook where the gentian bloomed is the southern terminus of the North Bay trail. This picturesque trail runs north from the parking lot at the overlook. It skirts the edge of North Bay, progressing through seven spectacular ravines, some steep and rocky, to the Stony Creek canoe landing, where it can also be accessed. From the landing the trail continues northward along Stony Creek, ending at Kidd Lane.

The entire trail from the parking circle to Kidd Lane is about a mile long, as measured on a map. That is a somewhat deceptive measurement; it doesn't take into account the numerous ups and downs, which add about another half mile. It can be easily hiked at one time, but I prefer to walk each section on different days, allowing ample time to observe, photograph, and enjoy the delights of nature in a leisurely fashion (See trail map).[2]

Lingering fog shuts out the distant view of the mountains.

Toward the end of the month, Lu and I drive to the canoe landing to meet Josh, a Bard College student who assists with my equipment. We plan to walk north to Kidd Lane along the more moderate of the two trail sections. The trail head is at the bottom of the bluff, just above the dock. The narrow path descends into the dark forest. The trees obscure the morning sun, and the forest feels damp and cold, as we scramble down the muddy slope over exposed roots and fallen branches.

Progressing through the tall trees and up a small hill, we emerge into a clearing. The bright light and warming sun are welcome. Stony Creek and North Bay are now visible on the west.

Sunlight edges tall trees through which the North Bay trail meanders.

We soon discover what created this open space in the forest. A large white oak tree with a mammoth root system, about twelve feet in circumference, has been uprooted and lies diagonally across the clearing. Wrinkled dry brown leaves are still clinging to the branches. We surmise that this forest giant was toppled several months ago in the heavy snow and tornado-like windstorm that swept through northern Dutchess County on April Fool's Day. The destructive storm blew down hundreds of trees in the Tivoli Bays uplands and the surrounding area.

Storms such as this April event are part of a normal pattern of disturbance in nature that generates damage and renewal at the same time. They create major changes in the forest and in the plants and animals that live within it. Many animal homes are destroyed; the lives of insects, mammals, reptiles, amphibians, and birds are often seriously disrupted. At the same time, sunlight pouring into newly created clearings, where the once shady tree canopies have been opened up by blow-downs, encourages the growth of different plants, shrubs, and tree seedlings. Different species of birds, insects, and other forest creatures come to live in the clearing. As the forest changes, it is strengthened by these new arrivals.

The upended oak tree with its roots exposed is a miniature ecosystem in itself. Although many creatures were driven out as it fell, it provides a bonanza of newly available food for chickadees, tufted titmice, and other insect-eating birds, which find eggs, larvae, cocoons, and adult insects in the network of roots. It offers a thousand little hiding places for salamanders and other small creatures, while chipmunks and squirrels scamper over the fallen giant, garnering acorns.

The leaves and twigs of the downed tree are home to another fascinating form of life. These are galls, peculiar growths created on leaves, stems, twigs, and other parts of living plants by three groups of minute creatures: mites, gall midges, and gall wasps. The insects, many less than one-eighth inch in size, seeking food and shelter, stimulate the tissues of the host plants to grow varied structures, called galls. Within the galls, the tiny creatures are provided with plant food and an enclosed home. Curiously, each of the 1500 or more different kinds of gall insects is usually restricted to just one kind of plant or one part of a plant.

Most walkers in the woods or along roadsides have seen galls, perhaps without knowing what they are. Some are as simple as a rolled-up leaf or a pouch. Many are very striking in shape or coloration, like the mossy rose gall and hedgehog gall of the oak. Willows on the marsh bank have galls resembling miniature pine cones. Goldenrods have swellings on their stems. There are blister galls, ball galls, bud galls, bullet galls, flower galls, leaf galls, leaf spots, roly-poly galls, root galls, rosette galls, stem galls, among others. They come in many colors: green, spotted-purple, pink, red, yellow, black.

On the ground are some dry, round, brown oak apple galls, about three-quarters of an inch in diameter. Each has a small hole in it, where the gall wasp exited in late spring or summer. Oaks, especially, are known for the great variety of galls produced on almost every plant part: roots, bark, leaf, stem, twig, acorn, and bud.[3]

In the sunlit clearing, goldenrod and purple asters

Green-headed coneflower is a typical composite.

are blooming. Like many of our familiar late summer and fall flowers, they are members of the large daisy family, and are known as composites. Each flower head is composed of numerous smaller flowers (florets), growing together in a tight cluster. Typical composites have flat petals in a circle around a center disk, as in a daisy. Sunflowers, coneflowers, ox-eye daisies, goldenrod, asters, sneezeweed, bur-marigold, beggar-ticks, and Joe-Pye-weed are among the many composites in the wetlands.

Beyond the clearing, the trail meanders through a

Oak apple gall

A tiny American toad rests on a clump of moss edging the path.

forest of tall oaks, maples, beeches, ash, and other deciduous trees. Red, yellow, and faint purple are beginning to tinge the leaves. Occasionally a red maple, also known as swamp maple, is entirely aflame with brilliant scarlet leaves.

In the understory, small sassafras trees display vibrant yellow leaves. Sassafras leaves come in three different shapes on the same branch or tree. Some leaves are shaped like mittens with one large lobe and a thumb; some leaves have three lobes; other leaves are oval with no lobes. Crushing a leaf produces a fragrant scent. This small shrub-like tree is the source of an aromatic oil used to scent soaps. Many songbirds and wild turkeys relish the sassafras berries. White-tail deer graze on the foliage and twigs, and cottontails eat bark and twigs.

The trail proceeds through a grove of tall evergreen hemlocks on a hillside. The ground under the hemlocks is almost bare, in contrast to the brushy understory of shrubs and herbaceous plants under the deciduous trees. Very little sunlight sifts through the hemlock branches, inhibiting the growth of the understory.

Alongside the path we note an unusual shrub-like tree with spidery yellow blossoms strung along its branches. It is a witch-hazel, which surprisingly blooms in late September or October, usually after the leaves have fallen. Witch-hazel is the only tree in these woodlands that has ripe fruit, next spring's leaf buds, and flowers on it all at the same time.

Along the trail lowly mosses and lichens are everywhere, blanketing decaying logs; growing on the bark, around the bases of trees, on the ground; creating colorful mosaics on boulders. John Bland, in *Forests of Lilliput*, writes that in mosses and lichens, "strength is mingled with humility, gentleness and charm . . . reflecting the gladness of wind, sun and rain . . . To know them is to feel a nearness to the texture of nature, a love of the lovely, and a sadness, too . . ."[4]

Lichens are fascinating in structure, shape, and function. Each lichen consists of an alga and a fungus growing together in a cooperative arrangement. The green alga manufactures food, and the layers of fungus provide moisture. Lichens are grouped into three types: crustose or flat; foliose or leafy and papery; and fruticose, either branching or stalked. They may be gray, green, yellow, black, orange, red, or other hues.

These unique little organisms are the first plants to take hold on a bare rock. They can survive in places where no other life exists: above the Arctic Circle, on barren mountain tops, in the desert, in the bitter cold of Siberia. They range in size from minute to massive. From ancient times to the present they have had many uses as food, for medicines, in medical research, and in perfumes, cosmetics and dyes.

In the clearing is a large boulder covered with an almost flat, scaly, pale green growth, a crustose lichen. Here and there on the rock are bright green mosses, diminutive cushion-like plants somewhat more advanced than lichens. All along the trail lush mats of leafy lichens with ruffled curling margins adorn tree trunks and rocks.

Colorful mushrooms and other fungi appear among the mosses and lichens. A stump nearby is covered with multi-colored "turkey tails," little fan-shaped fungi striped with brown, black, copper, and green bands. Another log has delicate one-inch round pink puffballs growing in the crevices. Elsewhere, leafy flowering plants and tree seedlings are sprouting on the mossy disintegrating logs. The woodsy smell of dampness and decay scents the forest air around us.

The trail now runs close to Stony Creek, where it tumbles over rocks on its way to North Bay. At one place a huge tree trunk stretches across from bank to bank, creating a bridge several feet above the creek. It's a neat highway for small creatures like squirrels, as well as sure-footed walkers, who want to cross to the opposite side. Farther on we hear the roar of water. The noise emanates from a spectacular waterfall in Stony Creek, unseen from our trail.

At the end of the trail on Kidd Lane, Josh offers to jog back to get his car at the canoe landing. Meanwhile, Lu and I walk a short distance east on Kidd Lane to the DEC entrance road, where Josh soon meets us.

A few days later, on a brisk thirty-degree morning, I meet friends to explore the rest of the North Bay trail, this time walking southward from the canoe landing. The path proceeds along the edge of the bay through the forest. Tohees, tufted titmice, and song and swamp sparrows call from the trees at the edge of the water, and raucous blue jays scream overhead. In the heavy layer of brown oak leaves on

The trail runs alongside rushing Stony Creek.

the forest floor, we find rock polypody ferns, remnants of jack-in-the-pulpit's red berries, and some large red-tinted mushrooms, the edges of the caps nibbled by mice or squirrels.

Openings in the forest provide varied vistas of North Bay. Great expanses of cattails, gold in the early morning sun, create meadows in the open marsh, with only small areas of sparkling water visible. The trail proceeds up and down hills, across a small ravine, and through a large hemlock grove. Beyond the grove we reach an incredibly beautiful ravine, the second of several. A small stream runs through it on its way to the bay, murmuring softly as it travels among huge slabs of rock. One large flat slab offers an easy bridge across the stream. To the west the brook widens into a small pool. Down in the shady glen are lush ferns, tall white boneset, pink smartweed, and other wetland plants. Small brown mushrooms, shelf fungi, soft spongy beds of green mosses, large mats of foliose lichens–all thrive in the moist environment of the ravine.

We discover an exquisite dragonfly with a black body and a three-inch wingspread, clinging to a dead branch. Its transparent wings, spread straight out, reveal a delicate network of veins with dark spots at each of the four corners. We suddenly realize that this beautiful insect is dead. Last night's cold snap had brought an end to its transitory life, reminding us that the passing of each season makes many changes in the lives of wetland plants and animals.

All the while that we walk, we hear continuous honking over the marsh and the river. The wild notes sound like the barking of distant dogs. The honking emanates from passing flocks of Canada geese, arrowing southward on their migratory flights, and tells us, as did the death of the dragonfly, that fall has arrived.

Scrambling up and down the next two ravines, we find ourselves on the edge of a high bluff. A magnificent view of North Bay stretches out before us. On the west is the straight line of the railroad embankment, interrupted by a red railroad bridge. A large pool is created by the tide as it flows under the bridge and fans out in the marsh, which is laced by an intricate network of creeks interspersed with patches of dense vegetation. Beyond the tracks the river and heavily wooded Cruger Island, against a backdrop of the mountains, are visible from our high viewpoint. The entire scene is framed by a kaleidescope of fall color on the trees clinging to the hillside.

The next ravine is very narrow, deep, and rocky. A tremendous fallen tree lies across the gap, but I don't feel quite agile enough to walk across it. Instead, I scramble down into the crevice and climb up a kind of steep rocky staircase on the other side. Farther on, I actually have to slide down another steep-sided ravine, the sixth, on the seat of my pants. The seventh ravine is somewhat easier to cross, and we soon reach the end of this picturesque trail. It exits from the woods at the northeast corner of the parking lot off Cruger Island Road.[5]

Lush ferns thrive in the moist environment of the ravine.

Panorama of Tivoli North Bay, Cruger Island, and the Hudson River is viewed from a high bluff at the junction of North Bay and Overlook trails.

Sulphur mushrooms on a decaying log on Cruger Island in fall

Puffballs and mosses on the moist forest floor

(Above): A garter snake is among the small creatures found on the picturesque North Bay trail, where lichens and mosses create a colorful mosaic on rock and log (right).

Lovely closed gentian, a rare flower in the region, was found blooming on the day of the fall equinox on the shoreline of North Bay.

Hoar frost in late October enhances bittersweet berries with fragile silver spires.

Sugar maple flaunts its orange-red autumn leaves against the dark green of hemlock along the Saw Kill.

Floating leaves and slender stalks of cattails are burnished by the morning sun at Stony Creek canoe landing in late fall.

A placid stretch of Stony Creek, one of two permanent streams
which flow into the Tivoli Bays, reflects autumn colors and blue sky.

Many ducks, like these mallards, stop over to feed in the bays during fall migration (above). Rushing waters of the Saw Kill cascade down the rocky gorge in a dramatic fall on the way to South Bay (below).

Wild rice is silhouetted by a flaming fall sunset on South Bay.

7 OCTOBER

The Autumn Island

The mention of an island usually conjures up a picture of a mysterious and isolated piece of land surrounded by water, a place that can only be reached by rowboat, canoe, or other craft.

But what about an island that you can walk onto from the mainland, over a manmade causeway through a swamp? Add to that the romantic thought that the causeway, built in the early 1800s, was once traversed by island visitors who came on horseback or by horse and carriage. Now the island takes on an even more fascinating aura. Mix in some interesting local legends, information about its prehistoric inhabitants, tales about Henry Hudson anchoring offshore to trade with the natives on his voyage up the river in 1609, historical accounts of the island's nineteenth-century inhabitants, a personal narrative of a secret wartime event presided over by President Franklin D. Roosevelt, and even rumors of barges bringing ingredients like molasses to the island, where they were picked up for Dutchess County stills during Prohibition in the 1930s.

Add to all this the island's natural beauty and ecological value, and you have a preliminary picture of Cruger Island, which today is an integral part of the Tivoli Bays Research Reserve. A heavily-wooded strip of land, encompassing thirty-two acres, exclusive of the adjoining swampy areas, it lies just offshore in the Hudson River between North Bay and South Bay. Cruger Island was once a true island when the valley was flooded by the melting glaciers of the last ice age that created the Hudson. It became linked to the mainland by natural sedimentation over the centuries, augmented by the manmade causeway.

An 1812 map of Rhinebeck shows that "Cruger's" Island was previously known as "Magdaline." An eight-acre wooded sandstone island in the river about a mile north of Cruger Island, also part of the Reseach Reserve, is now called "Magdalen;" before that, the smaller island was known as "Slipsteen," Dutch for "whetstone," referring to its shape; before that, "Goat Island." At a later date, it was called "Red Hook Island."[1]

Two small islets lie off the southern end of Cruger Island. The southernmost, South Cruger Island, comprising just two-and-a-half acres, was excavated by archeologists starting in 1947. They found many artifacts, especially rough stone implements, such as projectile points, knives, and hammerstones, and also unearthed hearths, pits, and burial sites.

dence, known locally as the "Castle," near the eastern end of what today is Cruger Island Road.

After passing through a number of hands in the ensuing years, Cruger Island was acquired in 1812 by Dr. John Masten

One burial site on the island's southern tip contained four

of Kingston, who built a house near the south end of the

skeletons, thought to be the remains of three adults and an infant. The findings, supported by other excavations on the north end of the main island, led to the conclusion that the island complex had been occupied by Wappinger and then Mohican tribal groups, which relied primarily on hunting and to a lesser extent on fishing.[2]

The rich post-European history of Cruger Island and the adjoining mainland starts with Colonel Peter Schuyler, an Albany merchant, who purchased it from the local natives about 1680. Granted a patent to the area by Governor Dongan on behalf of the British Crown, his holdings included most of what is now the Town of Red Hook. The middle portion of the patent, including Cruger Island, was sold to Barent Van Benthuysen in 1720, who erected a resi-

island. In 1835, Dr. Masten sold the island to John Church Cruger, whose name the island now bears. Cruger was a wealthy New Yorker, said to be a descendant of two early mayors of New York City, a father and a son, both of them named John. The early Crugers were ship owners; their prosperous business may have been the source of John C. Cruger's wealth, enabling him to purchase Cruger Island at the age of twenty-eight after the death of his wife, Frances, in 1835.

Cruger and his young son, Eugene, moved into the Masten house, which burned down a few years later. Cruger remarried in 1843, and with his new wife, Euphemia Van Rensselaer, and his son, they moved into a gardener's cottage in the middle of the island. Cruger added on to the cottage and orna-

Above: An 1860 view of the John Church Cruger house reveals Victorian embellishments. *Photograph courtesy Egbert Benson Historical Society.*

mented it over the years, creating a lavish three-story Victorian mansion for his growing family.

Among other embellishments on this island estate was a fake Mayan temple "ruin," which Cruger built on tiny rock-bound South Cruger Island to exhibit some authentic Mayan artifacts, given to him by John Lloyd Stephens, a New York City lawyer, adventurer, and writer. Stephens had led the first expedition to the jungles of Central America in 1839 with Frederick Catherwood, discovering the ancient Mayan ruins. A year later they returned to the Yucatan and brought back a boatload of Mayan antiquities.

Exhibited in Catherwood's Panorama in New York City, the sculptures were later destroyed in a disastrous fire. Only a dozen artifacts, delayed in shipping, remained in Stephens' possession. He gave these to his old friend Cruger, who shipped the massive limestone sculptures by river steamboat to his island home. Cruger entertained many visitors, and it is reputed that he often took them on moon-light cruises to view the Mayan treasures in the imitation temple on South Cruger Island.[3]

Cruger died in November, 1879. His body was borne on a funeral train to New York City, and he was buried in a vault under Trinity Church. His wife, Euphemia, died in 1888 and was buried next to her husband.[4] Two Cruger spinster daughters, Cornelia and Catherine, were said to have lived on in lonely isolation and poverty in the mansion until the early 1900s. A Cruger relative, Euphemia Van Rensselaer Wyatt, in an unpublished memoir written circa 1971, tells of visiting Cruger Island after the death of the elder Crugers. Mrs. Wyatt described the rundown condition of the house and grounds, adding "The one thing that remained the same was Cousin Cornelia herself, beautiful as ever in her well-worn black dress." Catherine died in 1914. Cornelia, becoming bedridden, was moved to a house in Annandale and died in 1922. The island was sold sometime before Cornelia's death in 1922, and the Cruger house was later torn down.[5]

The last arch remaining from Cruger's fake Mayan temple was photographed in 1960. *Photographer unknown.*

By 1998 only six crumbling fieldstone pillars were still standing on tiny South Cruger Island.

The Mayan sculptures were purchased in 1919 by the American Museum of Natural History in New York City, when Cruger Island and the adjoining mainland were briefly owned by a New York millionaire, L.G. Hamersley. I recently visited the museum to try to track down the sculptures, and surprisingly found these artifacts still on exhibit in the second-floor Central American gallery. Three magnificent heads of Mayan deities are prominently displayed on a large wall, identified as having come from elaborate sculpture facades of the "Nunnery" Quadrangle at Uxmal, Yucatan, and two massive sculptured slabs, or door jambs, are mounted on either side of a doorway leading out of the gallery. The accompanying museum plaque states that these pieces are of "special historical interest," as they were brought to New York in 1840 by John Lloyd Stephens "during his pioneering explorations of the Maya[n] area." Stephens and Catherwood, it states, were the primary discoverers of the ancient Mayan ruins. No mention is made of the fact that the sculptures were once exhibited on South Cruger Island.

In 1926 Hamersley sold the estate, including Cruger Island and his great gray Tudor mansion on the mainland overlooking the river, to Robert Boyd Ward, a prominent bread manufacturer. Mr. Ward conveyed the estate, known as Ward Manor, and money for its upkeep to the New York Society for Improving the Condition of the Poor for "the establishment and maintenance of a home for the aged, a home for convalescents, and summer outing camps" for working class families. Within a few years, two boys' camps were built on Cruger Island, and four girls' camps established on the mainland. Eighteen summer vacation cottages were built near what is now the Stony Creek canoe landing.[6]

The Tudor mansion and some surrounding land were sold to Bard College in 1960. The imposing gray stone edifice is now a college dormitory. Cruger Island and about 850 acres on the mainland were sold to the Central Hudson Gas and Electric Corporation, which planned to locate a nuclear power plant on the property. Fortunately, these plans were dropped, and the land, inluding the island, was sold to the New York State Department of Environmental Conservation in 1979. The island and the adjoining mainland, so rich in history, legend, and natural attributes, are inseparable parts of the tidal bays. The bays could not be a viable wildlife and research reserve without the uplands which drain into them and the island which helps to delineate North and South Bays.

Today Cruger's beloved imitation "ruins" on South Cruger Island are themselves in ruin; only a few crumbling stone pillars still stand, visible when the leaves have fallen. They can be viewed if one ventures out to the lonely islet in a canoe, as I did one chilly November day not so long ago. As I pho-

A century-old engraving of Cruger Island, with Cruger's house in the center, appeared in an 1880 pilot's guide to Long Island and the

tographed six tall fieldstone pillars, all that remains of the romantic Mayan temple reproduction, I felt that the little knob of land was haunted by the ghosts of John Lloyd Stephens and John Church Cruger, and by the Native Americans who had inhabited this same islet more than 4000 years ago, and whose skeletons had been unearthed nearby.

During the 1930s and '40s, Cruger Island and the river nearby were the setting for other interesting events. A longtime resident of the area told me that during Prohibition in the 1930s Tivoli Bays was known for "rum running." Dutchess County, he related, was full of stills, including one at Silver Lake, where the large copper vat is reputed to rest at the bottom of the lake. The liquor manufactured in the local stills, he said, was highly prized, and was taken in small boats out near Cruger Island, where it was loaded onto river boats to be transported down the Hudson to New York City.[7]

The most fascinating bit of history is the account of a top-secret demonstration of plywood landing craft that took place in the Hudson River off the island, just prior to our entry into World War II. Details of this event were related to me by John Carbary of Rhinebeck, now 83 years old. In the 1930s and '40s he was chauffeur to Lyman Delano, President Franklin D. Roosevelt's first cousin. Carbary said he knew the president well, and Roosevelt asked him to assist Roland Redmond, a wealthy resident of Tivoli married to Delano's sister, in the secret preparation for the presentation. "I was twenty-six years old, and kept everything to myself for a long time afterwards," Carbary proudly told me. His story follows:

In June, 1941, President Roosevelt, accompanied by Secretary of the Navy Frank Knox, Navy Admiral Ernest King, Secretary of the Treasury Henry Morgenthau, and other officials, came to Cruger Island to witness the test and select a model to be manufactured. The day before the presentation, Redmond and Carbury took several four-foot proto-types of wooden landing boats out to Cruger Island in Redmond's twelve-cylinder Cadillac, driving over the rough water-covered causeway. The demonstration was to take place on the east side of the island in a swampy area between Cruger Island and the railroad tracks. Carbary and Redmond even prepared a small beachhead there.

On the day of the demonstration, more than a hundred Army men were stationed all around the perimeter of Cruger Island, some facing out and some facing in, each in sight of the next man. Roosevelt and several officials came up the river in a PT boat to a landing spot about midway of the island on the west side. They were met by Army jeeps which transported them across the island to the east side. Other invited observers arrived by train in Barrytown and were driven out the Cruger Island

Hudson River. The engraving was captioned "View of Cruger's Island, from near Hog's Back buoy." *Engraving courtesy of J.W. Aldrich.*[8]

causeway.

Following the demonstration of the landing craft, the president and his top officials conferred at a big round table, which had been set up about fifty feet back from the shore. Carbary, Redmond, and others, including Henry J. Kaiser of Kaiser Aluminum Company, who had been invited to attend, stayed in a large tent near the shore.

When Roosevelt and the other officials had selected the landing craft which they planned to have produced, the president wrote a check for a million dollars to Henry Kaiser. When I asked Carbary how he knew the amount of the check, he said, "The president saw me near the tent and called out 'Jack, give this check to Mr. Kaiser.' He always called me Jack, but everybody else called me John." Carbary took the check from the president and gave it to Kaiser, who had been selected in advance to receive the contract for building the wartime plywood landing craft.[9]

☺ ☺ ☺

Intrigued by these exciting stories, I plan a visit to the legendary island, hoping to learn more about the lush forest which blankets it, and to seek some traces of its Native American and colonial occupants. Accompanying me will be Gretchen Stevens, a botanist on the staff of Hudsonia, to help identify some of the trees, shrubs, and other plants, and Dennis Mildner of the Research Reserve. Early one crisp October day, we drive out Cruger Island Road and the causeway through the tidal swamp, and park at the railroad tracks.[10]

Across the tracks, the causeway onto the island becomes a narrow path through overhanging shrubs and thorny branches. Here and there strands of spider webs are strung across the trail like fairy clotheslines, brushing our faces as we walk. The path soon widens and turns northward. Covered by a tapestry of fallen red, yellow, and brown leaves, it is

bordered by patches of attractive shiny green leaves hugging the ground. This familiar vegetation is periwinkle, the common evergreen ground cover also

Among the mosses, lichens, and fungi in the forest are puffballs (*above*), and mosses with spore caps (*below*).

known as myrtle or vinca. Last spring, when Lu and I visited the island, the periwinkle was abloom with little purple flowers, while overgrown forsythia shrubs, their branches arching above the periwinkle, were laden with sunny yellow flowers.

These domestic shrubs and flowers on a seemingly wild and isolated island are immediate reminders of John Church Cruger's sojourn here 150 years ago. Church loved flowers, and his wife, Euphemia, was said to be an ardent gardener. They created lavish sunken gardens near the mansion, as well as a swamp garden at the southwest tip of the island. A twenty-acre marsh there was reputedly diked in the 1800s and had a windmill to pump water for greenhouses in which Cruger was growing Italian grapes.[11] A pool in the northwest corner of this marsh has a luxuriant growth of yellow iris. Erik Kiviat surmises that it may have been the locus for the introduction of this European plant to the area.

The path we are following now was probably a carriage road, bordered by ornamental species. Although no longer groomed by the Cruger gardeners, the forsythia, periwinkle, and numerous exotic shrubs and trees have survived and seem to compete successfully with native vegetation. Gretchen points out some low shrubs with narrow, pointed oval leaves. "This is swamp leucothoe, or fetter-bush," she tells us. "It's a native shrub which has attractive sprays of tiny white bell-shaped flowers in late spring. It may be a survivor from the Cruger plantings."

I stop to inspect a fallen log, its textured surface deeply furrowed with horizontal ridges. Tiny mosses and lichens are tucked into the furrows. "Bird cherry" is Gretchen's instant identification of the log. "It's easy to distinguish from other wild cherries because of the horizontal ridges and lenticels, or pores," she explains. "It is an introduced species."

Continuing on the trail toward the northern tip of the island, we are soon surrounded by a mature forest of tall trees, mostly hardwoods. Gretchen

The crown of a tall white oak towers high over the forest.

identifies numerous trees: red and black oak, chestnut oak, and a few white oaks; sugar maples, flaunting fiery orange-red fall color, and red maple; hop hornbeam; some small beeches with clear yellow leaves. Other common trees we observe include black birch, basswood, black cherry, hickory, and eastern red cedar.

A pileated woodpecker carved these feeding holes.

We note a few beautiful hemlocks, their delicate short needles, silvery beneath, giving a soft lacy appearance to the branches as every breeze stirs them. Small brown cones, less than an inch long, hang gracefully from almost every branch and hide in the leaf litter underfoot.

Near the path is a very tall tulip-tree with a trunk as straight as a telephone pole. The tulip-tree is so named for its large orange and yellow-green flowers, appearing in May and June, which resemble tulips. Because the tree is so tall, the flowers are usually too high to observe at close range until they fall. The fruits are oval, hard, pale brown cone-like objects about three inches long. The broad leaves, a clear golden yellow in fall, have four lobes with a distinctive notch at the top. The tulip-tree is native to the eastern and central states. We speculate whether Cruger may have planted this specimen.

We are astounded at the great size of some of the trees. Gretchen and Dennis measure a large chestnut oak by stretching their arms around the trunk. They estimate that it is at least twelve feet in circumference–about forty-five inches in diameter.

Despite their size, the trees on the island are not "virgin," or "old growth," Gretchen says. "Most forests in the Hudson Valley have been cut more than once since European settlement, and uncut stands are virtually absent. Large trees like these with more than a century of unrestricted growth persist in many areas where they have been protected from cutting by inaccessibility or for other reasons." Cruger Island, she pointed out, has no signs of stumps which would indicate recent cutting. "This island, however, like many other Hudson River islands, is subject to natural disturbances such as high winds and fires that would cause changes in the forest succession."

Progressing down the path, we come across the massive sycamore which Lu and I admired when we were seeking the elusive golden club in the spring. Its trunk, like that of the chestnut oak, measures almost four feet in diameter. Its leaves, with five lobes edged with coarse teeth, resembling gigantic maple leaves, are strewn about the forest floor. Picking up a leaf, yellow and green in its fall raiment, I marvel at its size; the leaf is over ten inches across! The mottled brown bark of the sycamore flakes off in patches, revealing large and small areas of lighter grey bark and creating a kind of abstract crazy-quilt pattern. Parts of the trunk eventually become smooth and bare.

Standing under the big trees and gazing upward at their towering canopies, I feel dwarfed and awed by the power and beauty of nature in this nearly undisturbed setting.

Nestled in the fallen leaves are some strange hard brown balls about an inch in diameter, covered with little spikes. They are the fruit of the sweetgum tree. The sweetgum has symmetrical star-shaped leaves and corky wings on its branches. Locating the tree nearby, we admire its range of fall color. Some leaves are purple, others magenta. Other sweetgums might bear bright scarlet, golden yellow, or orange stars in autumn. Curious about the origin of its common name, I read later that a sweet gum exudes from cut stems; some people chew it, and it is used in perfumes and drugs. The first part of its scientific name, *Liquidambar*, is a poetic allusion to the sap. A native tree which grows southward from lower New York State to Mexico, this attractive tree is often used in ornamental plantings.[12]

Gretchen identifies a shrub whose leaves each have five leaflets, similar to our native Virginia creeper, as five-leaf acanthopanax, an introduced and rare plant. Here it grows profusely along the trail, a century or more after it may have been planted by the island's early occupants. Acanthopanax, along with fetter-bush and wayfaring-tree, is an uncommon escape from old plantings.

A graceful gull soars overhead as we walk.

These three do not ordinarily become invasive pests in this area.

Among other introduced plants that Gretchen finds on the island are oriental bittersweet, common buckthorn, false-indigo, tree-of-heaven, garlic-mustard, and Eurasian honeysuckle. False-indigo is common along the Hudson River shoreline but rare elsewhere in the Hudson Valley, she says. The other introduced plants are widespread in the valley, and considered significant pests in native forest habitats.

As we walk, Dennis points out the ring-billed gulls which have been flying overhead throughout the morning, migrating southward. He has also spotted a kestrel and a red-tailed hawk. A loud "kik-kikkik-kik" call pierces the air at that moment, answered a few minutes later by a similar call from farther away. "Those are two pileated woodpeckers talking to each other," says Dennis. Another series of somewhat nasal "yank-yanks" he identifies as a pair of white-breasted nuthatches.

By noon we reach the northern tip of the island,

where a colorful vista of the Hudson River and the shoreline greets us. Magdalen Island lies about a mile to the north, a rocky, rounded promontory crowned by trees in bright hues. We picnic on the little half-moon beach at the river's edge, enjoying the peaceful scene.

Dennis soon calls our attention to traces of prehistoric midden piles along the shore. Hundreds of pieces of crushed mussel shell are clues to the Native Americans who once camped on Cruger Island. As we follow the trail up a wooded hill to the west, more shell fragments are visible underfoot.

At the top of the hill, we find ourselves on a high rocky bluff overlooking the river and the Catskills. These ancient peaks are often referred to as "purple mountains," and today I understand why. The mountain range is a lovely muted purple hue, capped by a mosaic of fall colors and framed by blue in the sky above and the river below.

The trail winds southward along the edge of the bluff, and we pick our way carefully over tree roots exposed by erosion. Enchanting fairy gardens of mosses and ferns grow in the open ledgy habitats along the path. Gretchen shows us rock polypody, a small evergreen fern that can flourish on the thin soils of rock crevices; pale green "pincushion" moss that forms low, rounded cushions a few inches to a few feet in diameter; and lots of apron moss, or *anomodon*, a dark green moss common on the bedrock outcrops in this region. Nearby are numerous low shrubs with maple-like leaves that are a delicate shade of pale lavender-pink, accenting the greens of the ferns and mosses. The shrubs are maple-leaf viburnum, a common native plant.

Several yards off the path we detour to examine a marshy pond, lying jewel-like under the trees. Completely covered with an emerald carpet of duckweed, it is a favorite haunt of frogs and dragonflies in spring and summer. Gretchen reaches down under the duckweed and brings up a handful of tiny plants composed of minute ribbons. "This is an interesting liverwort, *Riccia fluitans*," she explains. "Unlike most liverworts, it is suspended in the water and is unattached. The Latin name *fluitans* means 'floating.' "

Liverworts grow in moist places—stream banks, damp soil, rotting logs—as well as on tree trunks and rocks. Some species are flattish and divided into lobes suggesting an animal liver, a trait from which this curious plant derives its name; others are leafy. Some liverworts form dense mats intertangled with mosses. Mosses and liverworts belong to the same division of the plant kingdom, the Bryophytes.

Leaving the pond, we continue on our walk, searching for the remnants of a brick fireplace and chimney I had come across a few years ago near the south end of the island. Reminded by Dennis that we have to get back to the truck before the next high tide makes the Cruger Island causeway impassable, we hurry along the trail, around fallen trees and up and down small rises. Two-thirds of the way along the west side of the island, Dennis, who has been scouting around, calls from the top of the bluff that he has discovered the remains of an old building. Hoping to find traces of some early nineteenth-century buildings, we scramble up the hill to a crumbling ruin almost hidden by the trees. A fifteen-foot portion of a windowless cement wall, about six feet high, runs along the ridge; on one end is an almost-intact arched brick entranceway. A cement floor is littered with bits of tarred roofing and other debris. Curiously, the floor slab is only about eight or nine feet wide, and the whole structure is perched precariously on the edge of a deep wooded ravine behind it. Later I learn that this is the remnant of a utility building for the Ward Manor boys' camp which was built nearby in the 1920s.

A tranquil view of the river and tiny wooded Magdalen Island can be seen from the northern tip of Cruger Island.

Mindful of the tides, we regretfully turn back. Our explorations today have revealed only a few tantalizing reminders of past human inhabitants and intensified the aura of mystery that pervades this storied island. The forest, however, with its mixture of native and introduced plants, has revealed its greatest strength to us: its incredible capacity for growth and survival over the centuries.

Faded green shutters provide open air siding for a duck hunter's blind in North Bay.

8 NOVEMBER

Duck Blinds
and
Deer Hunters

November in the tidal wetlands is a half-way month. The brilliant colors of fall have faded, while the winter snows have not yet arrived. The first of the month has dawned clear and very cold. It's twenty degrees at seven o'clock. When the temperature has climbed to a still frosty twenty-eight degrees by mid-afternoon, I drive out to South Bay to greet the new month. Most of the leaves have fallen from the trees in front of the Ecology Field Station, providing a clear view of the bay through the bare branches. A big flock of white gulls rests on the sandbar about a hundred feet from shore; farther out are three great blue herons. Herons often stay in the bays until hard ice seals off their feeding grounds, before migrating southward.

At the bottom of the path, the receding tide has left a wide band of debris from the decaying water-chestnut plants—leaves and mounds of bulbous stalks, covered with duckweed. The green bumpy carpet is interlaced with hundreds of black spiky chestnut hulls and a scattering of fallen brown, red, and yellow leaves.

Along the shore a crystal-thin layer of ice, pocked

with holes, glitters in the sun, and plates of the thin ice are upended against a fallen log. It is the first ice of the season, portent of the winter to come.

The leaves on the stand of wild rice just offshore in South Bay are turning yellow, although the stalks are still green. The nutrient-rich grains of rice that ripened in August and early September have long since been harvested by birds.

Wild rice is not a wild form of cultivated white rice but the seed of a different aquatic grass. Small stands grow in both North and South Bay. Farther north, in the marshes on the west shore of the river and in the Stockport Flats Research Reserve, wild rice is more abundant. A century ago, this grain grew on Manhattan Island and on Indian lands in upstate New York, but development has mostly obliterated it. Today, Native Americans still harvest it commercially in the Great Lakes area.

I have often wondered whether it would be possible to harvest wild rice locally, but found that the amount available is very small. In the estuary sites it ripens gradually over several weeks, so that only a tiny amount could be harvested at any one time. The wild rice in Tivoli Bays rightfully belongs to the birds.

Leaving South Bay, I drive out Cruger Island Road and walk along the Neck. The vegetation is very sparse now. The tidal creeks along the road, previously hidden by summer's lush growth, are clearly visible. Like South Bay the creeks are fringed with thin sheets of ice. Picking up a piece of lacy ice, I can see through it; it feels like a piece of fine crystal, and I am amazed that the force of the tides has not shattered it.

Nearby, despite the cold, a few pale lavender and purple asters are still bravely blooming, and great fluffy silver seed heads of clematis hang over the path, their stems twining around the leafless shrubs. Pale orange globes of bittersweet, prompted by the frost, have split open and turned back like wings, revealing the bright red berries inside. The brilliant orange, bell-like blooms of Canada lilies, which graced the causeway last summer, have been replaced by large woody tan seed pods.

At the overlook near the parking lot off Cruger Island Road the big pool in North Bay appears at first glance to be an expanse of muted brown, but soon many subtle hues unfold—rust and cinnamon, honey-beige, chestnut brown, straw and hay color. On the shoreline, oak leaves still clinging to the trees are leather-brown, mingled with a few lingering reds, and beech leaves are copper-brown. The great sea of cattails in the pool is a sensuous golden tan; a few brown spikes are tipped with silvery bits of fluff where seeds have burst out. In the low light of the late afternoon sun the entire scene is transformed into red-gold.

Feathery fronds of wild rice

About a half hour before sunset, hundreds of blackbirds alight on the trees with a great clamor and drop into the sheltering cattails, after a day of feasting in the stubble of nearby cornfields. The corn has long since been harvested, but random ears left by the corn picker, along with insects and insect larvae, are still available. The red-winged blackbirds, starlings, and grackles have been gathering in flocks since late August, leaving the wetlands daily to fatten up in neighboring fields before migrating in late fall. Each day at dusk they can be seen and heard, calling to each other noisily, as they return to Tivoli North Bay to roost for the night in the safety of the cattails.

Late one afternoon in November I join Dennis Mildner on the bluff overlooking Tivoli South Bay and the river. The sky is turning pink with a pre-sunset glow, as we wait expectantly in the frosty air. A small flock of blackbirds flies north over the river. Now there is only an empty sky. After a brief interval a few more red-winged blackbirds pass overhead, heading north. Suddenly the sky erupts with thousands of blackbirds in a great undulating black cloud, all flying north.

The pulsing waves of birds seem endless at first, until once again the flights slow to a trickle. Then another explosion of birds fills the sky, as thousands more weave overhead in a huge skein, heading for North Bay. We watch successive flights in awe as the sun sinks lower, and leave reluctantly only when our fingers grow too cold to hold the binoculars and the black throngs have dwindled to a few specks against the blood-red sky.

The evening flights continue until late November. One day the birds leave at dawn and do not come back at nightfall. The redwings, starlings, and grackles are on the way south to their wintering grounds. They follow the Atlantic Flyway, stopping to feed and rest in coastal marshes and wetlands en route, until they reach the swamps and rice fields of the southeastern United States. There they remain in large concentrations until early spring.

Now Tivoli Bays is quiet, except for the twittering of the birds that have stayed for the winter and the music of withered leaves and grasses rustling in the wind off the river. As the vegetation in North Bay dies back, some curious structures are clearly revealed, perched on the vegetated banks which criss-cross the open water. One box-like creation, resembling a huge wooden shipping container, leans at a crazy angle toward the water, tilted by the tides. The wooden shanty is open to the sky on top; a few boards nailed haphazardly across the front next to a rough door opening are sufficient to hold its weathered siding together. I wonder how long it will be before it collapses and slides into the mud.

This battered architectural curiosity is an old duck hunter's blind, one of about three dozen that dot the wetlands. They are fanciful structures, fashioned of old doors and shutters and posts, odds and ends of lumber and masonite, tattered tarpaper and chicken wire. Most are built on stilts to raise the floor above high tide level. Some are sparingly furnished with a bench, a deck chair, or an old car seat, and have full or partial roofs. Dried stalks of vegetation cling to the chicken wire; styrofoam cups, plastic jugs, soda and beer cans, and old plastic tarps often litter the floors and the surrounding area. Many have been long abandoned, while others bear evidence of recent use. Debris from disintegrating blinds is constantly being washed into the marsh mud. Some blinds, refurbished and repaired every

A geometric duck blind is hidden in the cattails.

year or two, may endure for many years.

The waterfowl hunting season is usually scheduled for October, November, and December, either continuously or with a closed period. The major species hunted in the Research Reserve, especially in North Bay, are mallard, black duck, green-winged teal, blue-winged teal, and wood duck. Canvasbacks are usually hunted on the open river. Only a limited number of ducks breed in Tivoli Bays in spring: black duck, wood duck, and mallards are the only three nesting species, but many other species are prevalent during spring and fall migrations.

Prior to the season, a few avid hunters can be seen in their squat flat-bottomed boats repairing and camouflaging their blinds. They may use stalks of loosestrife, cattail, common reed, red cedar, or other vegetation. Many hunters are careful and environmentally conscientious, but their blinds still damage the fragile ecology of the wetlands. The area around each blind is highly disturbed, vegetation is often severely damaged, and the surface mud is deeply

A disintegrating duck blind will soon topple into the mud.

The tides have long since washed away part of this structure.

trampled and becomes soft and oozy. This area is an ideal bed for introduction of invasive weeds such as purple loosestrife and common reed. When these camouflage materials dry out, the seeds fall on fertile mud. Patches of loosestrife and reed in areas otherwise devoid of these species in North Bay are sometimes the result of duck blind building. These plants compete with the native cattails, which are of prime value to small birds, such as the marsh wren, along with waterfowl, muskrats, and other marsh inhabitants, for food or nesting habitat.

Duck hunter's blinds have some positive aspects. Those that stand throughout the year provide shelter for a variety of animals and increase the diversity of the wetland animal community. Poking into a blind alongside Stony Creek—one of the few structures that is accessible on foot—I found it festooned with webs where spiders have taken up residence. In a dry corner of the floor was a cozy white-footed mouse nest in a pile of old cattail leaves. Numerous

birds—great blue herons, egrets, great horned owls, wintering eagles—perch on top of the blinds, and red-winged blackbirds, grackles, and song sparrows may use the blinds for nest sites or song-perches. Mallards and muskrats are known to nest in blinds, while raccoons have been found sleeping in them.[1]

The Tivoli Bays area has been a state wildlife management area, open for seasonal hunting, for many years. It received the additional designation as a protected federal-state Research Reserve in 1982. Hunting for waterfowl, deer, and other fauna continues to be permitted. A current regulation of the DEC, however, prohibits new duck blinds from being built; old blinds may be maintained and used.

North Bay has always been heavily used by duck hunters, although in recent years, as the numbers of ducks have declined, so too have the hunters. Old timers Frank DeZago and Owen Kinery, both of Rhinebeck, once avid river hunters, reminisced recently about duck hunting and building the blinds in the 1940s in Tivoli Bays, which were then known as the "coves."

"About fifty years ago, when we were kids, North Bay would be black with ducks in the fall. There were thousands and thousands of birds. They were incredible—diving ducks like broadbills, and puddle ducks, teals, mallards, wood ducks, black ducks," Frank reminisced. "Opening day was a big day, an annual event, always a fun day. We would go out Cruger Island Road, four or five in every car, and the road would be lined bumper to bumper with cars and guys. Everybody stood along the road and shot. It wasn't unusual to come home with shot in our pockets. The river was dirty then, but not nearly so dirty as it got later when I was in my twenties. Now it's cleaner, but the ducks are scarce."

Like many other conservation-minded hunters, Frank no longer hunts the river and its coves. He hunts what he calls the "potholes"—small ponds and marshes—for just a day or two each year.

"I was a teen-ager when the war was just start-

ing in the forties," Owen said, as he sat on the steps of his cabin with his dog. "There were lots of ducks in the cove. Blacks, woodies, mallards, canvasbacks, and redheads. Also the flight ducks—shovelers and bluebills.

Owen Kinery and his dog hunted duck in the "coves," as the Tivoli Bays were known, about fifty years ago.

"We had a big old rowboat that weighed about 300 pounds. Four or five of us would load the boat about 4 A.M. and drive the truck down Cruger Island Road. If the tide was high, the road would be completely covered with water. So we'd paddle right down the road to the railroad tracks. We'd put that heavy old boat on the tracks and slide it into the cove. Then we'd go out to one of those blinds. Everybody had their own blind. We made them out of cedar posts on the bank. We tied the logs together for the floor and camouflaged them with cattails. Our blinds were probably a lot sturdier than those today. We repaired them every few years. Cedar lasts quite awhile.

"One guy had an old single-barrel twelve-gauge shotgun. It kicked so hard, he got knocked right out of the duck blind. When we finished hunting in the blind in the morning, we would get in a canoe and go up into the little inlets and 'jump' the ducks.

"Then I went in the service. When I came back, ducks were beginning to get scarce. After awhile we stopped hunting in the cove. I haven't been to Tivoli Bay in twenty years."

After World War II, the waterfowl numbers declined precipitously, as both Frank and Owen noted. Ten years ago, ducks reached a near-record low. The breeding duck population in North America totaled just under thirty-one million in 1988, less than a fourth of the long-term average from 1955 to 1988. The loss of the prairie potholes to farming across southern Canada and the north central United States, the continent's prime duck-breeding area, was the major region for this decline. It was compounded by several years of drought.

Great egrets perch on a camouflaged duck blind.

Potholes, depressions left by the glaciers, once crowded the prairies. Filled with nutrient-rich rainwater and surrounded by sheltering grassy areas, they are critical feeding and nesting habitats for waterfowl. As farmers drained the potholes and plowed under the grasslands for farmland, the duck population crashed.

Reacting to the urgency of the situation, Canada, the United States, and Mexico signed a pact, the North American Waterfowl Management Plan, in 1985. In league with private conservation organizations like Ducks Unlimited and the Nature Conservancy, they began to restore prairie potholes and other wetlands, and converted millions of acres of farmland into grassland reserves. The plan also includes protection and restoration of waterfowl wintering grounds along eastern and western coastal wetlands, and bottom lands of the lower Mississippi Valley.[2]

This effort is paying off, aided by several wet years. The spring of 1994 marked the first successful duck breeding season since the 1950s and 1970s in the midwest and southern Canada. That year ducks began migrating in record numbers from the prairie regions to their wintering grounds in the south and southeast. The pattern has continued, and the numbers of ducks have rebounded spectacularly, according to the United States Fish and Wildlife Service.[3] The 1996 fall migration of waterfowl was the largest in over a quarter of a century, Ducks Unlimited reported.

With continued management and improved ecological practice across the continent, hopes for a long term recovery of ducks are high. Although Owen Kinery and Frank Dezago may never see the sky "black with ducks" again, nature lovers and hunters alike eventually may enjoy the sight of large numbers of woodies and teals, canvasbacks and mallards, pintails and other waterfowl in the tidal estuaries along the Hudson.

Since small game hunting and waterfowl seasons remain open for several weeks in the fall, it is wise to check the state hunting schedule before planning any marsh trips. Opening day and the first few weekends of the various hunting seasons usually find the most hunters in the area, but they are normally out in early morning and late afternoon, so walks can be planned for mid-mornings and afternoons. I take careful note of the approaching opening date of the regular deer hunting season, when caution will keep me out of the area for a few weeks. By observing these simple steps, my marsh walks are not affected by hunting seasons.

Nonetheless, I am torn at the thought of hunters in this peaceful protected area. Many men—and some women—seem to enjoy killing animals. I can't understand a person admiring the beauty of a deer or the grace of a flying bird, and then putting a shot through its heart. However, humans have always been hunters since the days of the earliest man. Originally it was a means of existence, a necessity for survival. Today it exists primarily as a sport. One can call it "sport," but, for some, is it also an expression of the violence and rage so prevalent in our culture today? In defense of hunting, I understand that where deer are concerned, it is a means of controlling the exploding populations. We have eliminated the wild predators, such as wolves, which once kept deer and other wildlife in check. Current land use and vegetation change have also contributed to the deer explosion. Today, their only predator is man. There seems to be little conflict between hunting and other uses, such as birdwatching, hiking, canoeing,

research, and education in Tivoli Bays, and so, begrudgingly, I accept it.

⊛ ⊛ ⊛

Late in November, on another twenty-degree morning, I awake to see a heavy hoar frost on every leaf, twig, and blade of grass. The sun is shining despite the cold; it should be a good day to visit the Research Reserve. We drive up the highway about nine o'clock, admiring the silvery frost on trees en route. North of the Kingston-Rhinecliff Bridge a milky-white fog lingers over the landscape. Along the Kidd Lane entrance road the hoar frost gives the trees, shrubs, and weeds a fantastic other-worldly appearance, more mysterious because of the silent fog that envelops everything.

At the Stony Creek canoe landing the marsh

A white-tailed doe pauses at dusk in the uplands.

appears ghostly and gray. We start slowly back, waiting for the fog to lift. Little by little, the sun breaks through, and its rays begin to fall on the frost-encrusted vegetation along the entrance road. Every feathery plume of dry grass, every twig, branchlet, and leaf on the shrubs and the intricately-shaped seed heads of asters, goldenrod, and other dying fall flowers glistens, backlighted by the morning sun.

The seed heads of the asters are fluffy silver balls, like fairy Christmas tree ornaments, composed of a profusion of tiny seeds, each seed wearing a frosty crown. The gray-green-beigy goldenrod heads, containing a multitude of lovely fuzzy balls, glow with icy lights. There are over a hundred different species of goldenrod native to North America. Even in a small section of this roadside there are several different varieties of this ubiquitous plant, some with full dense heads, some with smaller curling plumes, others with arching elmlike branches, each different shape highlighted by the frost.

A seed umbel of Queen Anne's lace curls into a little brown cup known as a "bird's nest."

At summer's end and in early fall, the deep gold and yellow flower clusters of goldenrod graced all the roadsides and trails in Tivoli Bays and the surrounding countryside, complementing the cerulean blue of the asters. Now the color has faded, and the seed clusters are covered with filigreed frost. If we wait awhile, we might see flocks of goldfinches descending on the goldenrod stems to devour the ripening seeds.

The once-white blossoms of delicate Queen Anne's lace, made up of myriad florets, have lost their minute petals and curled into brown cup-like "birds' nests." Each slender curled stem has a sunburst seed head on its tip. The birds' nests are coated with beads of silver. Here and there Japanese barberry shrubs display small ice-covered oval red berries, strung along the arching thorny branches like necklaces, while countless round rose hips on the multiflora rose bushes are similarly sprinkled with white.

Almost every flowering plant, nameless weed, and grass along the Kidd Lane entrance road and in the open meadow on its western edge, every nut and berry in the adjoining woodlands, each floating and emergent plant in the tidal waters of the open marsh, has produced seeds by late November. Out in the marsh, little green fruits on broadleaf arrowhead have turned to brown, and their seeds will soon be released. Swamp milkweed displays graceful delicate pods from which the seeds with their feathery appendages have dropped or blown away. The wild iris on the wet banks has large banana-shaped pods, which drop their seeds as the sections curl back. The tall spikes of the purple loosestrife are spicy brown; the seed pods encircling the stem are like little popcorn kernels. Seeds are miraculous in design, structure, and function. Within each is the embryo for a new plant of the same species. Though many of these plants will die back in the coming winter, their seeds will be dispersed across the fields, woodlands, and in the water of the bays, and will germinate in the spring to perpetuate each species.

A few dozen little beggar-ticks, shaped like miniature pitchforks, are clinging to my pants leg with tiny sticky appendages. Nearby, round burdock fruits, composed of hooked, bristly bracts, hang menacingly on their stalks, waiting to hitchhike to other localities on the clothes of hikers or the fur of passing animals. Minute dust-like seeds of purple loosestrife and other plants also hitch rides in animal fur, on clothing, or on the tires of vehicles.

Some seeds, such as those of jewelweed on

The seed pod of black swallowwort vine, related to milkweed, resembles an upside-down milkweed pod.

the wetland edges, are exploded from the fruiting capsules. Jewelweed is called "touch-me-not;" when the seeds are mature, a slight touch on the pod or a passing breeze will cause the seeds to shoot out. Other seeds, especially those of floating and emergent plants like arrow arum, drift to new locations, or drop directly into the tidal mud. Seeds with feathery appendages, like those of cattail or clematis, are windblown. Cattail seeds may also float or fall on the ice and be carried to another part of the marsh by tides when the ice melts. Seeds of wild grapes and countless berries, eaten by birds and other marshland creatures, are eventually deposited in droppings in other parts of the wetlands or in more distant places. Many tree seeds, like those of maple, ash, and tree-of-heaven (*ailanthus*), have winged fruits or keys and are borne on gentle breezes or wild winter winds to fall elsewhere in the uplands.

In the ancient Gaulish calendar, the month of October-November was aptly called Samonias, or seed-fall. The Celts designated November as the first month of the new year, celebrating the winter festival of Samhain on November first. Samhain marks the beginning of the winter or dark quarter of the year—the months of November, December, and January.[4] It seems strange to start the year with winter, but it is logical when one realizes that the growth cycle begins in winter, as cold prompts seeds to germinate in preparation for their emergence in spring. The natural world only seems dead in winter; it is resting and waiting for the light and warmth of spring to return.

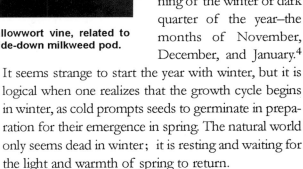

A chipmunk perches on a rock near its den.

9 DECEMBER

Where Have All the Creatures Gone

December is the month of the brightest moon, the shortest days, the longest night. Dumanios, the Celts called it, or "The Darkest Depths."[1] As the waning light and deep cold descend over Tivoli Bays and its plants and animals, the wetlands are transformed into another world.

Although the days are the darkest of the year, December nights are often the brightest. Winter moons are the most brilliant because they are usually highest in the sky and thus are dimmed less by the earth's atmosphere. My first journal entry for December 1990 notes that there would be two full moons that month, one on December 2, and another on December 31.

The moon will not only be full on these two occasions; it will also be at or near perigee.[2] That presages an abnormally high (and low) tide. What will happen in Tivoli North Bay this bright cold moonlit night, as a high tide moves up the estuary and sweeps into the open marsh? Will more wetland inhabitants than usual be up and about? Will coyotes sing under the full moon, owls hoot more loudly, and white-tailed deer and other wildlife find it easier to browse by moonlight than in the dark? Or will the brightness of the night keep small creatures in hiding, fearful of being spotted by predators?

Moonrise is scheduled for 3:40 P.M. on December 2, while sunset will occur a minute before 4:30. It should provide a dramatic spectacle: the full moon rising low in the east over North Bay, while the sun, a short time before setting in the west over the river, casts its unique end-of-the-day luminance over the marsh. My vantage point to observe this juxtaposition of sunset and moonshine on the tidal bay is the railroad causeway just south of Tivoli landing, offering an unobstructed view to both east and west.

The wind off the river is sharp, blowing at about fifteen miles an hour, but the afternoon is sunny at first. Shortly before moonrise, low clouds begin to form, partially covering the sun. The wind and the incoming tide have whipped up a strong current in the river; waves slap constantly along the shore. Not a single small bird is about; three gulls fly soundlessly overhead. The silent marsh lies before me, the tide flowing fast into the big channel, creating great ripples, while the waves in the river continue their

background beat.

The upland ridge behind the bay and the low cloud bank hide the beginning of moonrise. The sun is already starting to drop behind Magdalen Island in the river. My plan to photograph the special pre-sunset golden light on the marsh with the full moon rising behind it is doomed! But the sunset is radiant, as little Magdalen Island becomes silhouetted against the glowing sky, and brilliant pink and red are reflected in the river.

The sun sets behind Magdalen Island in the river.

I turn toward the east just in time to see a giant full moon lift dramatically above the forested ridge. It is still partially obscured by dark-gray clouds, trailing picturesquely across its pale yellow face. As the sun sinks lower and the sky darkens, the amber color of the moon deepens to a luminous saffron-gold, and an eerie light falls on the marsh.

A few sounds echo across the water: a dog barking on the west bank of the river; a hunter's gun, a series of far-off deep hoots as a great horned owl begins its nightly hunt. It is an unearthly moment as I stand alone in the darkening twilight, the sunset still glowing faintly in an almost black sky over the river behind me, the brightest moon rising in front of me, casting a shimmering pathway across the bay almost to my feet on the bank.

Elsewhere in the marsh, swamp, and woodland of the Research Reserve only a few creatures are stirring in the bitter cold of the long dark nights and the short days. Soon, when winter arrives in earnest, deep snows and ice will also descend on the wetlands, and there is a distinct change in the lives of most animals.

Walking the trails at this time of the year, I wonder what all the creatures are doing and where they have gone. The answer lies in many bodily changes which have been taking place gradually throughout the late summer and fall, as each species prepares in its own way for the approaching time of intense cold and limited food.

The most obvious way of avoiding the cold is to leave! The great blue herons, egrets, ospreys, ducks, some species of raptors, red-winged blackbirds, and a host of small songbirds that inhabit the wetlands in better weather have already migrated to warmer climates, flying hundreds or thousands of miles. Some creatures may travel only short distances to more favorable environments. The colorful little monarch butterflies, which danced over the cattails and the nectar-rich wetland flowers until late fall, have departed on their long migratory flight to Mexico.

Mute swans, Canada geese, and other waterfowl move down river to areas where the water remains open and food is still available, when ice seals North and South Bays and glazes the surface of the river. There is a small cove in the Hudson River near Peekskill where swans and geese congregate by the hundreds in cold weather; I watch for this annual gathering as I ride the shoreline train to New York City.

Some creatures, like Canada geese, move down river or migrate farther south.

The birds which remain in the bays for the winter, such as chickadees, goldfinches, cardinals, nuthatches, crows, woodpeckers, and jays, among others, utilize varying survival techniques. One adaptation is similar to that of the fur-bearing animals, which have developed heavy coats of winter hair and an extra layer of fat under the skin. Specialized feathers of the overwintering birds help to insulate them from the cold, and their intricate feather construction traps heat. Ruffling up their feathers also helps conserve heat. Birds and mammals alike use a mechanism familiar to humans: they shiver. The constant muscle movement generates heat. Watching the winter birds from afar in the frigid cold of the bays, I cannot discern a shivering response, but I observe the chickadees fluffing out their feathers. They look like tiny feather balls tucked away in sheltering niches on the lee side of trees, safe from the fierce winds that blow off the river. These tiny half-ounce birds, constantly on the move in the daytime, have another device for conserving energy. They lower their body temperature several degrees at night, in a kind of semi-hibernation which cuts down on the expenditure of precious fat and heat in the cold.[3]

Another great escape for a large proportion of Tivoli Bay animals is hibernation, an adaptation shared by many mammals, insects, reptiles, and amphibians. The main purpose of hibernation is to conserve energy. Among the warm-blooded animals of Tivoli Bays, woodchucks, raccoons, skunks, chipmunks, meadow mice, and little and big brown bats spend the cold months in a torpid or sleeping state. Some of these—the woodchucks, meadow mice, and bats—are "true" hibernators: they have almost no respiration, their heartbeats slow down to a few beats per minute, and their temperatures drop almost to the surrounding temperatures. They do not eat, drink, urinate, or defecate.

Other hibernating mammals of Tivoli Bays, like the skunks, chipmunks, opossums, and raccoons, are known as "shallow" or "light" hibernators. A major difference from the true sleepers is in their body temperature, which may drop only a few degrees, along with heart rate and respiration. They may emerge from sleep occasionally during the winter to take a stroll or hunt for food.

The perky chipmunk is among the "light" sleepers of the Research Reserve. A neat round hole in the ground is the doorway to an intricate underground chamber where the little mammal is spending the winter. To build its den, the chipmunk dug a sloping shaft about three feet down in the ground. At the end of the entrance tunnel it hollowed out several chambers, some for sleeping, some for food storage. In its cozy den, this diligent creature may have stored as much as a half-bushel of seeds, grains, berries, and nuts to sustain it through the winter. The chipmunk arouses from sleep regularly to eat from its well-stocked storeroom, and may come above ground from time to time on sunny days to check for uneaten acorns or leftover seeds.

The best known "light" sleeper of the mid-Hudson Valley is the black bear. No bears, however, are known to bed down in the Research Reserve; they hibernate in their home territory in the Catskills. Bears may awaken at times but do not eat throughout the winter, tided over by the great layers of fat they have stored up in the fall.

Other mammals of Tivoli Bays move about throughout the cold dark months. Food is harder to find; animals may have to travel farther in search of sustenance. The white-tail deer, the gray and the red fox, long-tailed weasel, ermine, eastern cottontail, white-footed mouse, and gray and red squirrels remain active in the snowy wetlands and uplands. The ermine or shorttail weasel has traded its brown fur for a spotless white coat as camouflage from its enemies. The squirrels seek shelter in hollow trees or in their leafy nests high in the tree tops; on unusually cold or stormy days they stay abed for long hours. In the fall, they bury stores of nuts and berries and are able to locate them, even under the snow, when they come out to eat.

Walking a snowy trail in Tivoli Bays, I find hints of hidden homes of other mammals that remain active but unseen

in winter. At my feet is an interesting rope-like mound of snow, the tunnel of a shorttail shrew. Only about four or five inches long, this tiny creature lives in a snow tunnel or in underground mouse runways in the cold weather. Extremely active, it requires tremendous quantities of food and forages constantly for worms, grubs, and insects under the snow. It supplements them with grains and nuts which may have been secreted by mice.

Another small mammal of Tivoli Bays which lives underground is the star-nosed mole. In warm weather its tunnel is just under the surface, but in winter this expert digger burrows deeper into the earth with its shovel-like front feet. Like the shrew, it exists on worms and insects which can be found in its tunnels.

While the mammals and birds are developing diverse techniques for survival, what is happening to the frogs, turtles, and other reptiles and amphibians that inhabit the tidal swamps, the bays, and small ponds? Snow and ice have sealed off their watery homes. Frigid air and silence reign where carp and mummichogs leaped, snapping turtles swam, and sound and sight of many insects filled the air a few short months ago. The aquatic residents of Tivoli Bays have devised their own modes of winter survival.

These cold-blooded animals also hibernate, traveling down into the muck at the bottom of the wetlands. The term, "cold-blooded," is a misnomer. The temperatures of reptiles and amphibians may be hot or cold, depending on the season and weather. In dormancy, their heart rate, respiration, and other bodily functions slow to the surrounding tempera-

White-footed mice in nest stay dry in a duck blind.

Snow and ice seal off the watery homes of reptiles and amphibians in cold weather.

tures. They require only a little oxygen. The frogs and even the large snapping turtles are able to absorb enough oxygen through their skin or other body parts to supply their needs, until spring arrives and they emerge from hibernation.

Another reptile of the Research Reserve, the

garter snake, seeks out a sheltered place on land where frost does not penetrate, such as a deserted animal burrow or other hole in the ground. There it spends the winter in deep hibernation. Snakes may congregate in large numbers to conserve moisture, sometimes intertwining in a large ball.

Most of the fish of Tivoli Bays spend the cold months in a sluggish or dormant state. Species like sunfish, bullheads, and white perch feed less in autumn and may not feed at all in winter, moving to deeper water, and taking shelter under rocks and logs. Some fish may take bait dropped through the ice by fishermen. The large carp, on the other hand, feed voraciously in early autumn and put on a layer of body fat. As winter approaches, they burrow into the mud and spend the coldest weather in a deep sleep. It is reported that carp have survived even when their bodies become encased in ice. Although many fish die in winter, some live to spawn in the spring.

The diminutive killifish, abundant in North and South Bays, are very hardy. They are able to withstand changes in water temperature which might destroy other fish. In winter killifish may go into deeper water, burrow into soft mud on the bottom, or become sluggish. Among the first to become active in early spring, they provide needed sustenance for hungry snapping turtles emerging from hibernation.

Following the rhythm of the seasons, insects too have disappeared from the tidelands and uplands as winter approaches. Although the air around us seems devoid of the countless buzzing, flying, biting, swimming, crawling insects of spring, summer, and fall, the winter wetlands are teeming with hidden insects. They survive the cold in various forms we may not see or recognize as they wait for the lengthening days and warmth of another spring to set the marsh abuzzing again.

Most insects go into a kind of hibernation called diapause. Like the frogs and turtles in the marsh mud, their metabolism—heartbeat and breathing—slows down, and they survive on stored glycogen and fats. Each species has selected its own distinct form in which to spend the time of cold: egg, nymph, pupa, larva, or adult. They may overwinter in crevices, in bark, under rocks, in leaf litter, in a rolled-up leaf, in

A cattail spike provides a cozy winter home for the tiny cattail moth caterpillar.

Promethia moth, also known as a spicebush silk moth, overwinters in a cocoon.

a hole in the ground, in the water, in other secret places. Unable to regulate their body temperature, they may be subject to freezing when bitter cold penetrates their hiding places. To guard against death, some insects have the ability to produce glucose, glycerol, and alcohols which act as a kind of antifreeze.[4]

Dragonflies and damselflies die at summer's end, but their progeny survive at the bottom of the marsh or swamp in a nymphal stage, the only part of their life that is aquatic, as described earlier.[5]

My favorite among all the overwintering insects of Tivoli Bays is the tiny cattail moth caterpillar. In late fall or early winter this minute creature, only a quarter of an inch long, finds a cattail with its seeds just beginning to fluff out. The caterpillar burrows into the spike, and as it goes from seed to seed to eat its fill, it spins a silken thread which ties the cattail head together. Thus it insures its food supply and a cozy blanket that the winds cannot tear apart.

Although protected from dessication and starva-

tion in their winter homes in the cattail spikes, the tiny larvae are no match for hungry chickadees. The birds flit from cattail to cattail and seem to know just which fruits to probe for a meal of caterpillars hiding within. In late February or March, returning red-winged blackbirds also seek overwintering insects in the cattails when other food is still scarce. The caterpillars which survive form pupae in the spring, and emerge as small moths in summer.

Other insects also seek shelter in cattail spikes and stems and in stems and parts of other wetland plants. Water-lily leaf beetles overwinter in the empty husks of water-chestnuts. On sunny summer days I observed countless numbers of these brown beetles with yellow edges on their wing covers, flying about and walking over spatterdock leaves, leaf rosettes of water-chestnut, purple loosestrife plants, and fading petals of the wild yellow iris on the bank. By midsummer, the water-lily and water-chestnut leaves are riddled with holes where the beetles have fed. They overwinter in leaf litter, mosses, and rotting logs in the forest, and in the stalks of purple loosestrife, as well as in the empty water-chestnut husks.

One day in late November, on the high bluff overlooking South Bay, I discover a small gathering of ladybugs in a cozy hollow on top of a big rock. The crowd of shiny little red balls with black spots, like a cache of miniature marbles, is convening in preparation for the long cold months ahead. These familiar insects are also known as lady beetles or ladybird beetles. In some places thousands of the bright spotted insects congregate with others of the same species prior to winter. They join forces, not for warmth, but to increase a foul odor emanating from their bodies, warning predators they are unpalatable because of an accompanying foul taste.

Ladybugs may cluster in an old stone wall, under leaf litter, in a hollow log, or other protected spot to stay in a diapausal state until spring. In some areas of the West, where they gather by the millions, they are harvested commercially to be sold to farmers and gardeners because of the ladybugs' voracious appetite for insect pests.

There are almost 500 species of ladybugs in the United States, distinguished one from another by the number of spots or lack of spots on their wing covers, colors, shapes, and other characteristics. They range in size from one-sixteenth to a quarter of an inch in length. They may be oval or spherical, and are somewhat flat from back to belly. Some are native, some introduced. Many are brightly colored in shades of yellow, red, or orange; others are black or tan. They may have no spots, two spots, or as many as fifteen spots, or irregularly-shaped blotches. A common ladybug found in Tivoli Bays, the twelve-spotted lady beetle, has ten spots on its attractive red wing covers, and two on its thorax.

Of all the countless species of insects, ladybugs are among the beneficial kinds. They are revered by gardeners and beloved by children. In spring and summer, they and their offspring, thousands of ugly black or gray alligator-like larvae, hatch from the minute orange eggs laid by the adults. The ladybugs are not all "ladies." Some are male, some female, and they must mate before the female engages in egg laying, unlike aphids which can reproduce without benefit of males. One female ladybug can lay up to a thousand eggs in a season.

The adults and larvae consume millions of aphids and other insects which attack the wetland plants. On farmlands, aphids feast on valuable food crops. Many years ago the European farmers dedicated the lady beetles to the Virgin Mary in gratitude for their services, and named them "Our Lady's Beetles." Many superstitions and myths surround the beetles. A lady beetle found in the house was considered an omen of good luck; killing one brought bad luck. They were reputed to bring good weather, good harvest, and romance.

Several years ago, the New York State legislature adopted the nine-spotted lady beetle as the official state insect. At the time it was thought to be common throughout the state, but research found otherwise. It has not been seen in New York State since 1970, possibly due to predation by an introduced Asian beetle, although it is common in the West.[6]

When spring comes, the sleeping hordes of ladybird beetles awake. They spread their filmy, transparent flight wings, which have been hidden under the hard spotted outer wing covers, and fly off in all directions through the wetlands. There they will assuage their ravenous appetites with aphids and other plant insects and start another cycle of beneficial eating, mating, and egg laying.

Ladybugs gather in groups to spend the long cold months.

Other wetland insects find different strategies for winter survival. The fat white grubs of May beetles, familiarly known as Junebugs, live in the ground for two or three years, digging deeper in winter as they enter diapause. The grubs of the introduced Japanese beetle, common in the Tivoli Bays swamps and uplands, also winter in the ground under grass roots. They spin their pupae underground in spring, emerging as adult beetles in summer. The larvae of the seventeen-year cicada stay underground for seventeen years. The spring of 1996 saw them emerge by the millions in a mass upward migration throughout the Northeast. These large nymphs provided a high-protein gourmet repast for birds and other creatures. Countless thousands survived, climbing up trees and plant stems to metamorphose into winged adults.

Many water beetles and bugs seen swimming in the marsh in summer, whirling crazily around like the whirligig beetles, or upside down like the backswimmers, or just floating lazily about, winter over as adults. Diving beetles, which may live for several years, hibernate in the bottom mud, becoming active toward spring. Water boatmen and backswimmers live through the winter by clinging to water plants or congregating in air pockets under the ice of the marsh and swamp. Others spend the cold months in diverse ways.

Last summer a very large football-shaped hornets' nest hung low from a tree branch over a bend in the Stony Creek channel in North Bay. It was head-height. We had to be careful to avoid it as we rounded the bend in our canoe; a head-on collision could be disastrous! What has become of the hundreds of hornets in the hive as winter approaches? The nest, composed of layers of thin gray papery material, which the hornets manufactured by chewing up rotted wood, will offer little protection from the freezing atmosphere.

When the nest was being constructed, the queen laid the first eggs in the papery cells. These eggs produce larvae, which are fed by the queen until they develop into workers. The workers feed the new larvae, as additional eggs hatch. By summer's end, males and females develop from the larvae and mate; the females become new queens. The old queen, the thousands of workers, and the males die in autumn, their duties completed, their short sojourn in the marsh ended.

Now the new young queens leave the nest to seek shelter in disintegrating logs, under fallen trees, and in other protected niches around the edges of North Bay. There they spend the winter in diapause. When warm weather arouses them, each queen will fly off to find a tree branch and start construction of another nest. A new generation of bald-faced hornets will soon proliferate in the wetlands.

The great nest, now the funeral bier of uncounted numbers of bald-faced hornets, hangs over the channel for most of the winter until the winds tear it apart. Tattered pieces of the gray paper layers are scattered along the snowy paths. A nest in a more

Millions of seventeen-year cicadas emerged from their long underground stay in the spring of 1996. *Photographed under controlled conditions.*

sheltered place in the forest may survive the winter intact. Then it can be taken down and cut open. Inside are row upon row of combs, divided into individual cells, each open on the underside, many containing dead hornets. Be aware that a few may have survived!

The month winds down to December 21, the day of the winter solstice. It dawns cold and somber with no snow. At the overlook off Cruger Island Road, everything is a monochromatic gray. Despite the dull atmosphere, I feel a surge of joy. The winter solstice marks a distinct change. It is the turning point of the year. Tonight all the plants and animals of the wetlands will experience the longest night and the return of the sun. As winter begins, a little more light returns each day, ensuring the resurgence of all living things by spring and summer.

On this day of the winter solstice, looking out over the marsh, I know that the darkness will gradually end. I feel a strong connection to the rhythms of the natural world, and to the wetland animals whose lives are intricately bound to these rhythms—to the sun, the moon, the tides, and the eternal cycle of the seasons.

A large hornet's nest hangs over the Stony Creek channel.

Great ice floes, split apart by the tides, line the shore of South Bay in mid-winter.

Fluffed-out cattail plumes reveal a delicate beauty in the dim light of a winter's afternoon.

Red-winged blackbirds return to the wetlands as early as February, the jaunty males arriving well before the females.

Snow powders bushes and covers drowned logs in the tide swamp along Cruger Island causeway.

Wrinkled woody shelf fungi and evergreen ferns add color to a stump on Cruger Island in the midst of winter.

By January, snow and ice have locked up the Stony Creek canoe landing, while winter cattails create

a border of beige and gold on the frozen tide channel, and a vast quiet reigns over the marshlands.

Myriad cattail seeds surround the base of a cattail stalk on the frozen marsh. When the ice melts, the seeds will float to a new location.

The fruiting stalks of last summer's sensitive ferns, also known as
"bead" ferns, poke up above the snow that blankets the wetlands.

The never-ending tides still course up and down the icy Hudson River in winter. The tip of Magdalen Island appears at the left.

10 JANUARY

The Time of Cold and Ice

In the ancient Celtic world, the month of December-January was known as Riuros–The Cold Time, "when the cold bites deep."[1] January indeed is the cold time in the Tivoli Bay wetlands. Not only does the ice bite deep, but in many winters the snows bite deeper. When Arctic weather blasts down the icy Hudson River and sweeps into the bays and coves along its shore, life in the ice-bound wetlands is profoundly changed.

One day in early January, Lu and I set off for a walk to observe the effects of winter in the marshes and uplands of the Research Reserve. Although the temperature is a cold twenty degrees, the day is clear and sunny with just a light coating of snow on the ground. We start out on the picturesque Saw Kill trail, which descends from Blithewood Road on the campus of Bard College and runs alongside the steep rocky ravine through which the Saw Kill rushes down to Tivoli South Bay. The Saw Kill is one of two permanent streams that flow into Tivoli Bays, meeting the oceanic tides that surge up the Hudson and into the bays. The other is Stony Creek, which flows into North Bay.

The trail proceeds through a young forest of red and white oak, red maple, white pine, hemlock, and other trees. Farther down, we encounter some very large hemlocks and pines, their great trunks deeply furrowed. They are surviving remnants of the old estate trees that once filled the area. Large logs, decaying on the forest floor, attest to others that have not survived the decades.

The only sound is the gurgling of the creek, growing louder as we approach a small waterfall. The sparkling water drops down through ice-bound banks into a plunge pool eroded into the creek bed. Below the waterfall, a concrete dam stretches across the creek, impounding a lovely pond. Rebuilt about thirty years ago, an original dam at this site may have dated back many decades. It was once a mill dam, one of many along the Saw Kill, wherever fast water operated sawmills, gristmills, and textile mills in the last century. In the early 1900s, a water-powered chocolate mill operated upstream on the Saw Kill, just below Annandale. Remnants of the mill are now part of a Bard College faculty house.

The mill pond above the dam is smooth and calm

today, partially covered with ice. In warm spring weather you may see dozens of painted turtles sunning themselves on the logs which poke out of the water, and if you sit quietly on the bank, you can observe numerous birds, dragonflies, and other wildlife in, around, and over the quiet water. In the chill of this wintry day, only a few chickadees are flitting about in the trees and in the dry vegetation on the shore, as they forage for food. These diminutive birds survive the cold and snow while other birds have long since migrated south.

Nick Hales / Historic Hudson Valley

The historic mansion of Montgomery Place across the Saw Kill

Across the creek are the North and South Woods of Montgomery Place. Towering hemlocks, huge sugar maples, and great oaks still stand in this forest that has not been cut for two or three hundred years, unlike the trees on the Bard lands where the trail runs.

Montgomery Place is an historic estate, recently restored by Historic Hudson Valley and open to the public from early spring to Christmas. The property includes a gracious twenty-three room Federal period mansion on a bluff overlooking the Hudson. It has formal gardens and naturalistic landscaping, along with an actively cultivated orchard of 5000 apple, pear, and peach trees. The mansion was built in 1804-05 by Janet Livingston Montgomery, daughter of Revolutionary War patriot, Robert R. Livingston, and widow of General Richard Montgomery. Montgomery Place is a fitting neighbor to the college campus across the Saw Kill and the adjoining Research Reserve, creating an unbroken stretch of preserved and undeveloped lands along the river from the hamlet of Tivoli south to Annandale.

Continuing down the trail, we stop to examine the mammoth decaying logs. They are hosts to many fungi, lichens, and mosses. Small patches of snow lie under the trees, revealing a thick fibrous carpet of oak leaves, which decay very slowly. Earthworms, busy creatures that help break down the tons of debris that fall on the forest floor, seem to dislike oak leaves, perhaps because of their high acid content.

In the nooks and crannies at the base of standing trees are little caches of nibbled acorns and pine cones devoid of their seeds, left by red squirrels as they dig into their winter stores. A bare trunk of another tree reveals an exquisite tracery of delicate lines etched into the wood by bark beetles. With her artist's eye, Lu discovers many other small wonders in the winter woods, and we both exclaim in delight as a streak of sunlight falls on the first green shoots of a skunk cabbage poking up through a patch of snow.

Farther down the path, a high hissing sound, accompanied by a low rumbling noise, precedes our

Ice-covered rocks add to the dramatic beauty of the lower Saw Kill waterfall.

first glimpse of the lower waterfall of the Saw Kill, dropping more than thirty feet down the steep rocky ravine. Frozen spray and ice-covered rocks add to the beauty of the falls in winter. This incredibly dramatic fall is "one of the most exciting natural features of the Bard campus," Erik Kiviat has written in a guide to the trail: *Mills and Minnows, A Walk Down the Saw Kill.* "Here, over 8,000 years or so since the recession of the last glacier, the creek has cut down through clay and rock to create the modern ravine."[2]

Below the waterfall, the trail descends to the wide mouth of the Saw Kill, where it flows into South Bay. Stretched before us is the broad flat expanse of the ice-covered bay, with the enduring misty mountains on the west. A vast quiet reigns. Only a few dry thin stalks remain from the summer's luxuriant growth of wild rice. The dense carpet of water-chestnut rosettes that covered the cove from June to September decayed in early fall, adding to the detritus on the bottom of South Bay. All along the shore are hundreds of hard black spiky water-chestnut husks washed up by the tides.

We follow the trail around the shoreline and up onto the forested bluff above the bay. On the hillside, the trees grow aslant, leaning toward the water as though some giant hand had pushed them sideways when they were saplings. These "tipped" trees give silent witness to the gradual movement of the soil down the bluff.

We stop to examine an old white pine, its bark shaped into square plates and riddled with little woodpecker holes in horizontal rows. The holes are the borings of a yellow-bellied sapsucker as it drilled the tree to extract the sap. Up in the tops of three tall oak trees are some large ragged nests, loosely constructed of twigs and leaves. These are the homes of gray squirrels, a familiar mammal in the Tivoli Bays uplands, active year around. In January or February they will mate and den up in a hollow tree. Baby squirrels are born in March, and in spring will scamper down the trees from high in the canopy and learn to forage for seeds, acorns, berries, and other food on the life-giving forest floor.

Lu and I soon reach a small high finger of land jutting out over South Bay, a favorite spot to rest and enjoy the tranquil scene below us. In contrast to the bustle and activity of spring and summer on the bay and in the forest, the only sound is the delicate noise of water under the ice and the occasional grinding of ice floes against the shore, as the outgoing tide tosses them about, helping to scour the bottom of the bay.

As we rest, the silence surrounds and soothes us. "The silence is something positive and to be heard . . . a fertile and eloquent silence. The silence rings, it is musical and it thrills me," Thoreau wrote in his January journal.[3]

Gazing out over the bay, as the afternoon draws to an end, we become immersed in the solitude. The scene is pure enchantment—an expanse of ice with a thin layer of soft pitted white snow on top, a great jagged slash of silvery water running diagonally across the bay where the smooth surface of the ice has been ripped open by the ever-moving tide, the setting sun beginning to turn the entire bay to gold instead of white and silver.

Driving home at dusk after our long walk and peaceful communion with the winter beauty of South Bay, we are confronted by a great golden globe of a full moon rising low in the east, so large and

A jagged slash of silvery water runs across South Bay where the tide has ripped open the ice.

round and yellow against the darkening sky it looks as though it is cut out of construction paper and pasted in the heavens. Lu warns, "Don't take a picture of it. It's too unreal. No one will believe it."

A week later, Dennis Mildner offers to accompany me to Tivoli Bays to look for wintering eagles and other birds on the river. Dennis is an expert ornithologist, and I look forward eagerly to our expedition. The day of our trip dawns bitterly cold and windy. At 8 A.M. the temperature is eighteen degrees, with a wind-chill factor below zero. There is no snow, and fortunately the sun is shining as we start out in a DEC truck. Driving out Cruger Island Road, instead of walking, my usual mode of travel, is pure luxury in the bitter cold. En route we spot two magnificent wild turkeys, but see no other sign of wildlife. Low tide makes it possible for Dennis to drive through the rocky break where the tides flow across the causeway. The tidal swamp bordering the road is choked with ice, and mammoth plates of ice have been upended by the moving tides among the battered reeds and broken cattail stalks. Fingers of woody brush along the narrow rough road claw at the sides of the truck as we make our way slowly out to the railroad embankment along the river.

Dennis parks at a vantage point between South Bay and the river. Our attention is immediately drawn to some ducks in the river, and braving the sharp wind, we leave the truck to get a better view. A large raft of about a hundred ducks is stretched out in a dramatic long line on the water. Noting their white bodies and dark heads, Dennis identifies them as canvasbacks, along with a few buffleheads and a common merganser. Nearby, in the lee of South Cruger Island, four statuesque mute swans swim slowly, also seeking food in the open water.

The cold wind soon drives us back into the vehicle, where we have a good view across a narrow

The tide creeks in the swamp off Cruger Island Road are laced with ice.

channel of water to South Cruger Island. On the little island are some very tall "eagle" trees with stout limbs and open canopies. These trees are a favorite resting and perching spot for wintering bald eagles.

While we scan the tree tops with binoculars, Dennis explains that overwintering waterfowl and bald eagles are the most visible and active forms of wildlife that struggle to survive the bitter winter along the Hudson estuary. Farther south, resident peregrine falcons also stay throughout the cold months. Ducks begin congregating on the Hudson during November and stay to about the end of February. These include several species of bay (diving) ducks, like the canvasbacks, which can exploit what little open water there is to dive for food. Dabbling ducks, such as mallards and black ducks that normally feed on submerged aquatic vegetation in shallows, are infrequently seen, due to the extensive ice and snow covering in these areas.

"The bald eagles come down out of Quebec and Ontario to forage in upstate New York's lakes and ponds and rivers, as their summer breeding territories become locked in ice," Dennis relates. "When at last these smaller bodies of water begin to freeze, they move farther south onto the tidal Hudson, which is slower to freeze. As the fresh water areas of the river also begin to freeze, the eagles concentrate in areas like South Bay, when open water is available, and hunt it from the eagle trees. When even these pockets of water become locked in ice, the eagles move to the brackish lower Hudson. There the Iona Island Research Reserve near Bear Mountain becomes the focus of their activity. In deep winter, this area is critical to their survival. The ice cutters which continuously ply the Hudson's shipping channels in winter also keep the ice pack loose, providing open water for the avian hunters."

One eagle strategy is to sit in a tree with a good vantage point. Eagles need open water to hunt or scavenge for dead or dying fish, their preferred diet. They may also take waterfowl, either dead or diseased and slow. They are true opportunists, according to Dennis. Eagles hunt from a perch during the most severe parts of the winter. Most hunting activity takes place early in the morning; then they loaf on their perches most of the day in an effort to conserve energy. Sometimes they hunt again before they go to roost for the night.

Since early in the century, few bald eagles had wintered in New York State, but now this once endangered species is beginning to return in greater numbers. Peter Nye, chief biologist of the New York State Department of Conservation's endangered species program reported that 175 bald eagles, with seventy-five eaglets, were recorded in the state in the winter of 1997, compared to forty-one in 1979. The Hudson River, especially, is becoming a popular eagle habitat.[4]

In mid-April of 1997 an exciting and historic event occurred. The first eaglet birth documented along the Hudson River in a little more than a hundred years occurred on an island in the river in Greene County, about twenty-five miles north of Tivoli Bays. An eagle pair had been nesting there unsuccessfully since 1992, and it was thought that toxic elements in their prey might have been the cause.

The nest has been closely monitored by the DEC since 1995. One day a watcher observed one of the adult eagles catch a large fish in the river and bring it to its eyrie almost seventy feet up in a mammoth cottonwood tree, a probable sign that it was feeding young.

A few weeks later, Nye climbed up to the bulky nest. There an eight-inch-tall fluffy gray eaglet growled at him, while Nye collected samples of half-

These two injured bald eagles are being cared for at the Hudson Valley Raptor Center.

eaten prey to test for toxic contaminents such as PCBs. At the end of May, Nye repeated his climb, bringing the now six-week-old eaglet down to the ground for closer inspection. The bird was weighed, tagged, and photographed, and blood samples were taken before it was returned to the nest.

The eagles' past disappearance as breeding birds on the Hudson was probably due to loss of habitat and to human disturbance and industrialization along the river in the early part of the century. Shooting, trapping, and egging, removal of nest trees, and "very likely an increased use of pesticides, indirectly causing sterility in adult eagles that have fed on contaminated fish" contributed to the decline in the eagle population, John Bull reported in *Birds of New York*.[5]

There are no records of eagles having nested on Tivoli Bays, but it has good potential, with its isolated lowlands free of human disturbance and many good nesting trees. "There is a supra-canopy of white pines—old trees poking up out of the hardwood forest on Cruger Island and the uplands along South Bay. These are the types of trees eagles prefer," Dennis tells me.

While Dennis discusses eagles, we keep our binoculars trained on South Cruger Island and the sky above it. Our vigil is rewarded after about an hour, when an adult eagle flies up above the island, and in a few minutes is joined by another. We watch them for about ten minutes. The two birds spiral high up into the clouds and are soon lost to our sight. We drive slowly back over the Cruger Island causeway, feeling that our early morning expedition has been a success. I especially am the richer for it —not just because of the brief sighting, but because Dennis has provided me with a great deal of fascinating information about bald eagles, which have made the Hudson River their wintering grounds.

Although many birds migrate southward when winter descends on the wetlands, the ice-bound marsh and swamp interlaced with open water and the uplands of the Research Reserve provide shelter and food to a number of species. A watcher in the winter wetlands may see or hear jays and crows, woodpeckers and nuthatches, chickadees and titmice, cardinals, perhaps a few red-winged blackbirds that have stayed the winter, and many others. A tiny olive-gray bird with a whistle-like call and a bright yellow crown, a golden-crowned kinglet, may be seen, along with winter finches, such as the purple finch and the goldfinch, no longer bright yellow but a lovely chestnut brown in its winter garb.

A flash of heavenly blue is an overwintering bluebird, New York's state bird which not too long ago had almost disappeared from the region. It favored hollow nesting trees which were taken over by starlings or cleared for development. The proliferation of bluebird nesting boxes in open fields, set out and tended by bird lovers like the members of Dutchess County's Waterman Bird Club, has helped to reestablish this lovely songbird.

Snow and ice create an abstract pattern on North Bay.

Occasionally I catch a glimpse of the crow-sized pileated woodpecker with its flaming red-cockaded head. A walk along the Kidd Lane entrance road often scares up a ruffed grouse, while whole coveys of wild turkeys stalk unafraid across the road. I once counted twenty-two crossing in front of me and melting into the brush on the other side. There seemed to be three females and many younger birds, perhaps three families flocking together for protection, food hunting, or communal child care.

A red-tailed hawk may scream overhead, or sit quietly on a tree branch waiting for a mouse or other small creature to come out of its winter hideaway. The red-tail is observed frequently in the Research Reserve, while northern harriers and Cooper's hawks occasionally may be seen hunting the snow-bound wetlands.

Of all the birds in Tivoli Bays in winter, I am fondest of the owls, not seen as often as heard at dusk. Owls have always been of interest to me. For many years I collected owls on my travels: a Florentine glass owl from Italy; a carved cedar owl from Canada; two prized pewter owls that once were chocolate molds, found in the basement of an old candy factory; an antique brass owl from a flea market; and many others. My closest acquaintance with owls came at the Hudson Valley Raptor Center in Stanfordville, where I have spent many hours taking close-up photos of orphan baby owls, owls being rehabilitated after collisions with cars, and birds suffering from gun shots, pesticide poisoning, or other injuries. As I photographed, I learned the natural history of owls from co-director Dona Tracy and owl expert Julio de la Torre, ornithologist and naturalist, a frequent visitor at the Raptor Center. De la Torre's text for a photographic study of owls by noted wildlife photographer Art Wolfe is a fascinating source of information.[6]

Screech owls are also known as shivering owls.
Photographed at the Hudson Valley Raptor Center

Great horned owls, barred owls, screech owls, long-eared owls, and saw-whet owls are all found in Tivoli Bays. It's a thrilling, if somewhat scary sound, to hear the very loud, very deep hooting of a great horned owl nearby, as I have, when I was on the edge of Tivoli North Bay at dusk.

Owls have held a strange fascination and fear for mankind since the Stone Age. The earliest representation of a bird by man was a snowy owl, engraved on the wall of a cave in France 15,000 years ago. These myth-laden birds of the night have appeared in the folklore, literature, and religious and medical practices of many cultures. Their nocturnal habits create apprehension, and their weird shrieks, screams, maniacal laughter, eerie hoots, and human-like sounds startle and make one shiver. The British ornithologist, Edward A. Armstrong, in his book *The Folklore of Birds*, says that people are apprehensive of anything which appears to have human characteristics without being human. In most of the world, the owl is considered a bird of witchcraft, death, and doom. The appearance of an owl on a house or in nearby trees was an omen of death in Britain and in other countries. Conversely, the owl also foretold births, and contrary to its evil attributes, the owl is considered a paragon of wisdom. In Greek mythology, the owl was the symbol of Athena, the goddess of wisdom and knowledge.

Owl cures for many diseases appeared in ancient medical practice. Because owls are noted for their nocturnal eyesight, owls' eyeballs, if eaten, Armstrong recounts, would help one see in the dark, and because owls hoot and whoop without harm, owl broth was believed to be a cure for whooping cough. Superstitions regarding owls abound, even today.[7]

Owls have several very special adaptations that set them apart from most other avian species. Huge and brilliant, owls' eyes are very large in proportion to the owls' body weight and size. The eyes, facing forward, are set close together in the front of their disk-shaped faces. Owls cannot move their eyeballs, but instead can rotate their heads 270 degrees so they have a 360-degree view of the area around them. The eyes are sensitive to the faintest bit of light, enabling them to detect the tiniest movements of a mouse or other prey on the ground below them. The owl can't see in total pitch-black darkness, but relies instead on its acute sense of hearing to locate its prey. Its hearing is even more remarkable than its unusual visual ability.

The leading edges of the wing feathers of most owls have very specialized fine teeth, thought to mute the sound of air rushing over their wings, enabling them to fly in absolute silence. The naturalist, John Burroughs, describing owls, wrote, "All the ways of the owl are ways of softness and duskiness. His wings are shod with silence, his plumage is edged with down."[8]

The combination of acute sight, hearing, and silent flight makes owls the deadliest of predators. Their prey ranges from insects to small and medium-sized mammals. They do not chew their food, but their digestive system enables them to separate out fur, feathers, bones, and other indigestible parts of their food, which are later regurgitated in the form of gray fuzzy pellets.

If you want to find an owl pellet, first locate an "owl tree," a tree which an owl uses as a roost or nest site. This will be characterized by "whitewash" or droppings on the trunk or ground. In Tivoli Bays, old pine and hemlock trees are favorite owl roosts. Look under the tree for the little gray elongated bundles, ranging from less than an inch to three inches long. Owl pellets can be picked apart with a forceps, revealing skulls and bones and claws of small creatures, a clear

The barred owl is the source of many eerie hoots and weird sounds. *Photographed in the Everglades.*

record of what an owl has eaten.

One evening at dusk, Dennis and I ventured out to see if we could call up some owls in the woodlands near Tivoli North Bay. Armed with a taped recording of screech, barred, and great horned owl calls, we trudged through the shadowy woods and took up our vigil under the tall leafless trees. Dennis turned on the tape to the screech owl call, and the quavering descending wail echoed eerily through the woods. Screech owls, tiny creatures smaller than a robin, with either gray or reddish feathers, do not hoot, unlike most other owls. In parts of the south they are called "shivering" owls.

Repeating the taped call at intervals, we waited patiently. The first bird to appear was a cardinal in the branches overhead. Suddenly a deep-pitched loud resonant series of five low hoots, off in the distance, reverberated through the forest. A great horned owl was answering the screech owl! We listened almost with trepidation as the great raptor continued to answer the screech owl calls for about twenty minutes. Would this great "feathered king of the woods," as Angus Cameron dubbed him in *The Nightwatchers*,[9] come closer in search of a screech owl tidbit? Would it attack us?

The great horned owl is one of the largest and heaviest American owls—a fearsome creature about two feet tall with a wingspread of forty-eight to fifty-five inches. It sports two great tufts of feathers or "horns" on its head. According to de la Torre, the great horned owl is probably the most successful predator in North America. It prefers rabbits, rats, and mice, but will take opossums; woodchucks; muskrats; squirrels; large birds like grouse, geese, swans, and herons; many smaller birds; other owls; hawks; and fish.

To our disappointment, the owl did not come closer, and after awhile its deep hoots ceased. We played tapes of barred owl and great horned owl calls, but no other birds of the night answered. Barred owls are frequently heard in this area. They are known as "eight hooters." Their most familiar calls are two groups of four hoots each, ending in a decending "Who-oooo," often described as "Who cooks for you? Who cooks for you-all?" Barred owls are also the

The great horned owl is a fearsome creature. *Photographed at the Hudson Valley Raptor Center.*

source of a great variety of cackles, hisses, wild screams, barks, howls, and crazy laughter, no doubt giving rise to many stories of lost souls and strange human-like creatures wandering in the woods.

Although we didn't call out any other owls on our owl prowl, it was a magic night. An orange gibbous moon rose high above the trees, casting a pale light over the forest. Early in the evening a pair of northern harriers flew in tandem low over our heads, and pairs of Canada geese sailed overhead at intervals, calling loudly as they made their way to North Bay to roost for the night.

That winter evening in Tivoli Bays will long remain in my memory, with the haunting calls of the owls, both on tape and in reality, echoing through the darkening and lonely woods.

Late afternoon shadows fall across a snowy path off Cruger Island Road.

11 FEBRUARY

Winter Wanderings

February in the wetlands is often a fickle month, with wild swings from springlike thaws to frigid days, and mild rains to blizzards. Looking over my journals for the past several years, I find entries like these:

February 1, 1989: "A springlike day. Temperature up to sixty degrees. The winter woods are beautiful without benefit of snow. The land formations are revealed through trees devoid of leaves . . ."

February 3, 1991: "It feels like spring in the air, but winter is still underfoot, despite temperature in fifties. Ground is frozen. It's hard walking over the icy causeway to Cruger Island . . ."

February 10, 1995: "First day out to Tivoli Bays after a twelve-inch snowfall earlier in the week. All roads into the Reserve buried in deep snow. Impossible to walk without skis or snowshoes . . ."

In February 1997, my notes indicate that there was fairly mild weather almost all month. Average temperature was thirty-two degrees on February 3, twelve degrees above normal. The only snowfall was two to three inches on February 19, melting quickly in bright sun with the temperature rising to fifty. February 21 saw a high of sixty-five degrees with rain

showers; it plunged to eighteen degrees the next day, while the remainder of the month remained mild.

On the first of February a few years ago, a welcome continuation of a thaw at the end of January promised temperatures up to sixty degrees. I walk slowly down Cruger Island Road, my camera hanging like a heavy pendant around my neck. I wonder whether the hibernating animals might be tempted by the weather into cutting short their long rest, but not a frog or turtle is stirring. It will be late March or April before the lengthening days rouse them from their sleep. February 2 is Groundhog Day. However, no woodchuck in its right mind ever came out of its burrow this early, except when unwillingly aroused by dignitaries trying to prove the truth of the old superstition that if this creature sees its shadow, there will be six more weeks of winter.

Except for the temperature, it is still winter in the tidal swamp along the Cruger Island causeway. The ebbing tide is exceptionally low this balmy afternoon. Layer upon layer of ice, usually treacherous and slick, left by freezing nights and built up as successive tides flow across the Neck, is soft and crumbly. I can walk

Massive cakes of ice, tilted by the tides, line the river and the causeway in late winter.

without fearing for life, limb, or camera. In the tide creeks on either side of the trail are massive cakes of ice, some twenty- to twenty-five feet across, some crazily tilted by the force of the tides. Some are marked with delicate swirl patterns, painted by the wet brush of the tide across the ice, while wide zig-zag cracks filled with black water create an abstract pattern.

As I near the railroad tracks, a tremendous cacophony of bird sound emanates from the direction of South Bay. Curious as to the perpetrators of all this discordant noise, I am drawn southward along the railroad right-of-way. Looking across the bay, still mostly ice-covered, I am overwhelmed by the sight of an enormous gathering of gulls. As many as a thousand or more are massed several hundred yards from the shore. They call. They shriek. They squeal. They gabble, bark, and chuckle. They quarrel and are alternately noisy and quiet. Little groups of about a dozen birds take off from the crowd at intervals, wheel gracefully about, dipping or soaring on their slender but powerful wings, and land again on the ice. The quarrelsome crowd reminds me of a gigantic town meeting where everybody is attempting to talk at once and no chairman can gavel them down. I wonder what problems of bird-dom the gulls have under discussion.

From a distance I note that they are mostly white. A majority of the birds on South Bay today have gray "mantles" across the upper surface of their backs and wings. The wing tips are black with white spots. This raucous asssemblage is probably composed mostly of ring-billed gulls, although I can't see the identifying black ring around the beak without binoculars. Ring-bills are the most common gull in Tivoli Bays. Some herring gulls, also numerous in the bays, are probably part of this crowd. These two species are similar in appearance, although the ring-bill is smaller and more dove-like.

The herring gull is one of the two largest species of gull found in Tivoli Bays. It has a wingspread of four-and-a-half feet. Only the greater black-backed gull, found in lesser numbers in our area, is larger, with a wingspread of almost five-and-a-half feet. The herring gull is the bird most commonly referred to as the "seagull." The term seagull is really a misnomer; while these birds used to congregate mostly along the coasts and in harbors where fishing vessels came to unload their catch, some have always lived inland.

Gulls are primarily scavengers, eating almost anything except plants. At the seashore, when this resourceful bird finds a mussel or clam, it may fly up forty or fifty feet and drop it to smash the shell and eat the insides. In today's waste-oriented society, garbage dumps have drawn many of them away from the coasts. Gulls now can be seen in great numbers at inland shopping centers and malls where their diet of fish is being replaced by pizza crusts and hamburger remnants from the overflowing dumpsters.

I recognize one much larger blackish bird among the gulls: a double-crested cormorant, easy to distinguish by the S-curve of its neck and the erect pose as it stands upright on an icebound stump. He is the only silent bird among all the squawking gulls. Cormorants are nearly voiceless, although Erik Kiviat reports hearing them make low-pitched groaning calls, and Roger Tory Peterson writes that they make "pig-like grunts in nesting colony."[1]

I recently came across an odd little ditty about cormorants in a charming booklet, illustrated with a woodcut from Thomas Nuttall's *Manual of Ornithology* (1832-34):

"He paints his rocks a gleaming white,
The better to be seen at night;
Then dives for fish, and not in vain,
Returning soon to paint again."[2]

In my eagerness to photograph the gulls, I almost join them in South Bay. Trying to get as close as possible, I step out with one foot on a huge ice floe that is hugging the shore. Part of the floe, succumbing to the warmth of the thaw, suddenly breaks off. As my foot plunges into the mud on the edge of the bay, I sit down abruptly. Fortunately, there is another ice cake resting on terra firma directly behind me. I quickly shift backwards onto it, rescuing myself and my camera from an icy dunking while I wiggle my foot from the muck.

Fascinated by the gulls, I spend another hour watching them wheeling, gliding, or holding themselves almost motionless in the air, while others rest on the ice or float in an area of open water. Just before five o'clock, the entire flock rises, as though at a signal, and flies off in gradually receding waves.

In other colder winters, when the ice on South Bay is thick and smooth as glass, a protected area at the south end near the hamlet of Barrytown becomes the scene of a different gathering. The species on the ice this time is human instead of avian. They are the ice boaters, a hardy tribe whose members delight in the most frigid weather, preferably clear days with a stiff wind blowing and no snow.

The sport of ice boating was born on the Hudson River near the end of the nineteenth century when the Hudson River Ice Yacht Club was founded by the millionaires who lived along the river from Hyde Park to Catskill. Ice boating died out after World War I. It was revived in the 1960s and became a sport for local residents, according to Richard (Ricky) Aldrich, who is an avid participant. The barns at Rokeby, the ancestral Aldrich estate on the Hudson River south of Tivoli Bays, where Ricky Aldrich still lives, harbor a collection of the venerable ice yachts, some restored, some in various stages of disrepair. The flagship of the Rokeby fleet is the massive *Rip Van Winkle*, forty feet long, which Aldrich sails on the Hudson whenever a frigid winter locks up the river and the ice is clear and thick.

The Ice Yacht Club is still in existence, and its members have rescued and lovingly restored many elegant nineteenth-century wooden iceboats. When the ice reaches a thickness of six to ten inches, several of these classic vessels can be seen on Tivoli South Bay, along with a few smaller modern iceboats with brightly colored sails. "We started using South Bay in 1970; it's protected and freezes before the river," Aldrich explained.

The restored boats are massive beauties with highly varnished wooden frames, cotton sails, and cast-iron runners. They measure twenty-five to fifty feet from stem to stern. According to Reid Bielenberg, commodore of the Ice Yacht Club, a boat named *Icicle*, built in the 1860s for John Roosevelt, President Franklin D. Roosevelt's uncle, was over sixty-five feet long and was the fastest and biggest ice yacht on the river for many years. Bielenberg called it the "queen of the river." In 1885, John Roosevelt had a new boat built, also called the *Icicle*, about forty-eight feet long and twenty-eight feet wide, with 730 square feet of sail. On exhibit at the Roosevelt Museum in Hyde Park for many years, it now reposes at the Hudson River Maritime Center in Kingston.

The *Jack Frost*, given as a gift by President Roosevelt to Aldrich's father in the 1930s, is fifty feet long. It was restored in the 1970s and sails from time to time on the river. "It's too big to be hauled across the railroad causeway into South Bay, as are some of the other big ice yachts, so we keep a second fleet on the river," Bielenberg told me.

It is a thrilling experience

Restored nineteenth-century ice boats in full sail are ready to speed across South Bay.

just to watch from the shore of Tivoli South Bay when the right conditions bring out the iceboaters. The scene looks like a Victorian painting, with a small crowd of boaters and their friends gathering around a huge bonfire on the ice. "Traditionally, we often have big pots of pea soup on the fire, and the soup freezes on the spoon," Commodore Bielenberg said, remarking that the ice boaters have many good times. Their boats stand under full sail nearby, while a graceful craft or two may already be zig-zagging across the bay. When the wind is right and the ice thick and smooth, these beautiful craft hurtle across the bay at fifty to seventy-five miles an hour or faster.

The clear ice also attracts skaters, children on sleds, and dogs. The cove at the south end of the bay becomes almost crowded with people, while the gulls convene their meeting on a more isolated expanse of Tivoli South Bay.

⊛ ⊛ ⊛

When snow falls in February, as it normally does in a typical winter, walking the Tivoli Bays trails may become difficult but rewarding. A silence descends on the wooded uplands, the frozen marsh, and the swamp, broken only by the snapping of a twig, the crunch of my footsteps on the snow, the groaning of a tree when the wind blows. I feel a silent communion with the natural world on a snowy day.

As I walk one day among the tall pines and old locust trees on Cruger Island Road and thence along the narrow road that traverses the tide swamp, the snow, which had been floating lazily down, begins to fall more heavily, and a sharp wind blows. At first gentle, the swirling flakes become a thing of wild beauty. They whirl angrily around my face, give ghostly shapes to small shrubs and weeds, and deposit jaunty caps on birds' nests and tree stumps. Soon every twig and branch is etched with white.

When I reach the overlook at the South Pool on

The snow creates ghostly shapes on weeds and shrubs.

North Bay, the landscape is rapidly disappearing, receding into a white mist. Still visible near the shore, the winter cattails wear peaked hats on their ragged brown plumes, while an old duck hunter's blind across the pool is only a vague shape looming up through the curtain of snow. The sky to the west is a monochromatic gray; the Catskills are completely obscured.

On the ground at my feet where a cattail stalk pokes up through the snow, many minute feathery cattail seeds, shaken from the fat fruiting plume by the wind, lie lightly on the crystalline surface. The falling snow will soon blanket them. When the snow and ice melt, and the tides lick at the base of the cattails, some of these fragile seeds will be swept out into the marsh. A few may take root to help perpetuate the lush banks of cattails that are all-important to the ducks, muskrats, insects, and a host of other fauna which feed upon them. I picture in my mind a spring morning when an engaging little marsh wren will alight on the tip of a cattail stalk to sing its melodic song and dart off at intervals as it gathers downy cattail fluff to line its nest.

The snow continues, now heavier. My footprints are already obscured, as I turn from my solitary contemplation and walk back through the stillness to the van.

Wandering on other winter days around the edges of the bays, along the railroad right-of-way, or on the Cruger Island causeway through the tide swamp, I see very few mammals. They are shy or furtive, and many are nocturnal. Deer appear from time to time. Once I caught a glimpse of a coyote, and several years ago I spotted a red fox at the water's edge in the early dawn. The ubiquitous gray squirrels, on the other hand, are highly visible. The smaller red squirrels, which also inhabit the uplands, are seen less frequently. On warm February days a chipmunk may appear momentarily near the entrance of its underground chamber. Occasionally an opossum, with its pointed elfin face, pink-tipped nose, beady eyes, silvery gray fur, and long rat tail, might be sighted as it searches for food. The opossum, the only marsupial in the United States, has in recent years extended its range northward. It first crossed the Hudson River about 1920 into eastern New York State, but it doesn't cope well with extreme cold.

When snow covers the trails, a walker may find clues to many other animals that inhabit the marsh, the swamp, and the uplands. Hal Borland, in his delightful handbook to the wonders of the natural world, *Beyond Your Doorstep*, writes that "snow is the blank page on which you will find the tracks of most animals."[3]

Few animals venture out immediately after a nighttime snowfall, so I usually wait twenty-four hours before starting out on a tracking expedition. Then another world appears—the world of night and the creatures that roam the wetlands at dusk or after dark. They leave many kinds of tracks and signs, not just those made by claws and paws in the snow or mud: chewed twigs, a clump of

fur, rubbed or gnawed bark, a strong scent, droppings or scats, feathers, owl pellets, woodpecker borings in a tree. The tracks and signs reveal many marshland secrets and stories, as I try to learn what animals have been out, where they have gone in their search for food or exercise, what or whom they have found and eaten.

One year toward the end of February, after an extended snow-free period, three or four inches of snow fell and remained on the ground. With the temperature about sixteen degrees and rising gradually, Lu and I plan a short tracking foray into the wetlands. Suitably protected from the cold, we park at the Bard College campus. Cruger Island Road stretches ahead of us, an unbroken snowy path through the woods and the tide swamp. There are no human footprints or tracks left by cross-country skis or snowshoes. Perhaps it is too early in the morning or too cold for any but intrepid marsh walkers like us. Along the road, the branches of tall white pines with their soft green needles, the grey and black trunks of the hardwoods, and clumps of dry winter grasses are garlanded in snow. Overhead, the sky is turquoise, and the trees look more majestic than usual against the whiteness of the snow.

As we walk down the road, we begin to see tracks of creatures which were out at dawn before us. In deeper snow the tracks might have been hard to decipher. A few inches of snow on the ground or a very thin layer on a hard surface like ice or a rock provides the clearest prints. In several places numerous little holes in a helter-skelter pattern pock the snowy path. Puzzled at first by the strange marks, I suddenly realize that the "tracks" are caused by bits of snow dropping off the low-hanging branches and needles of the pines. Even trees leave "tracks!"

A little farther on,

Red fox

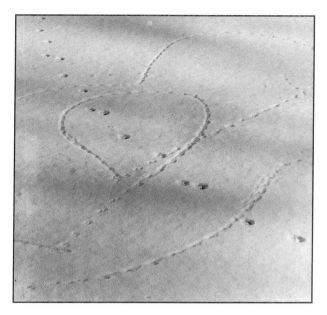

A mouse made this lacy valentine in the snow.

White-tailed deer leaves a deep hoof print.

Leaping red squirrel places hind feet ahead of front feet.

**A raccoon left these prints, like human hands,
in the mud on Cruger Island causeway.**

numerous deer tracks criss-cross the road. These are the footprints of white-tailed deer, the species that inhabits the eastern and central states. The larger mule deer is found primarily in the west. The white-tail is a very common mammal in Tivoli Bays, especially in the uplands, and it frequently enters the marsh and swamp. Easily identifiable, the tracks clearly show the deer's two-toed cloven hoof. Each toe is somewhat pear-shaped, and the two together create a distinctive heart-shaped print. Where the track is very clear, two small round prints made by the dewclaws can be seen at the base of the track. (Dewclaws are vestigial digits not reaching to the ground on the foot of a mammal.) Deer tracks vary in size; those of a doe might be two and a half or three inches long, while the tracks of a buck might be four inches or more. The fawns, which are born in February, leave one-and-a-half to two-inch prints. In deep snow deer tracks appear as large round holes. If there are several inches on the ground, a deer may leave a trough punctuated by round depressions of the hooves as it lunges through the snow.

Deer also leave other telltale signs: a mound of droppings, consisting of elongated tan or brown pellets about a half-inch or more in length; lower branches of trees that have been browsed, especially on hemlocks and cedars; a clump of fur caught on a branch. Once, following a deer trail into a forested area, I came across a deer bed where several animals had spent the night under the shelter of the trees. The snow was packed down, and rounded-out body forms showed me where deer had slept. Frequently, when I am out at dawn, I hear an animal crashing through the brush and get a glimpse of the upturned white tail from which the deer gets its name, as it disappears into the woods.

A different set of tracks, this time delicate paw prints almost in a straight line, lead out of the woods and cross the trail, disappearing on the other side. The prints, about two-and-a-quarter by two-and-a-quarter inches, similar to those of a small dog, are probably the tracks of a red fox. A clearer track might have shown claw marks revealing four toes. Unlike a domestic dog, this wild member of the canid family puts one foot in front of the other when walking, making a neat straight line, while our dog friends leave alternating tracks in a ragged fashion. Gray fox tracks are similar to those of the red fox, although smaller. Coyote tracks are larger, in an alternating pattern like dog tracks. Fox, dog, and coyote, all members of the dog family, usually show claw marks in their prints. Cat tracks, on the other hand, such as those of the domestic cat and the bobcat, do not reveal claw marks, as all cats retract their claws. Cat tracks also appear in a nearly straight line, like those of the fox.

On the side of the path we come across a dainty embroidery of tiny tracks around the base of a clump of snow-covered weeds. Each minuscule print in the thin layer of snow under the sheltering weeds is about a quarter of an inch in length; the four feet of this invisible creature leave a four-square pattern, with the slightly bigger prints of the hind feet in front of the smaller prints. The tracks of leaping and hopping animals such as mice, red and gray squirrels, and rabbits have the larger hind feet in front of the forefeet. The little white-footed mouse, which left the lacy tracks under the weeds, wandered around the weed stems for awhile. Perhaps it was searching for seeds. The tracks encircled the weeds, went ahead for about a yard, and then mysteriously disappeared. The mouse went under the snow, dug a tunnel, and plugged up the entrance behind him! The diminutive animal may have been alarmed by the shadow of wings above him or other sign of a predator.

Near the South Pool of North Bay we flush two

ruffed grouse. As they rise into the air with loud wing beats, we are almost as startled as they are. The trail they leave behind shows not only three-toed tracks but faint marks where their wings brushed the snow when they took off in sudden flight.

From the viewing platform overlooking the bay an incredibly beautiful sight awaits us. The pool is frozen solid and engraved with many swirls, ripples, and patterns in the ice. These too are tracks, tracks that tell a story of the ever-moving tides, the winds that blew over North Bay during the night, and a drop in temperature causing a quick freeze which preserved the tracks for awhile. In the distance stand the mountains, purple and blue, striated with white bands of snow; above them is the turquoise sky, and trailing across the sky below the grey and white clouds is another track—the long, faint trail of a jet.

Tracks and signs found on other snowy day walks or in spring and summer in the marsh mud have revealed other animals that frequent the wetlands—meadow voles, short-tailed shrews, raccoons, great blue herons, ducks and geese with their webbed feet. When you go tracking in Tivoli Bays, you might want to carry along Olaus Murie's *Field Guide to Animal Tracks*. This classic illustrated guide not only will be an aid to identification in the field, but also makes fascinating reading at home for the armchair naturalist.[4]

Sometimes I find it more interesting not to decipher the maker of tracks. Tracks set the imagination swirling, and it is intriguing simply to think about the unknown creatures going their silent ways in the winter woods and wetlands, making strange hieroglyphics in the snow. Then I can conjure up all sorts of creatures that come out after dark or at dawn, or hide unseen in the shadows as I walk. They are part of the magic and mystery that pervades the wetlands.

Delicate lines and swirls on the icy bay are tracks etched by the tides and winds.

Red-winged blackbird on a loosestrife branch sings behind a curtain of cattails.

12 MARCH

Return of the Blackbirds

March is the month that marks the return of the blackbirds to Tivoli Bays. To me, the returning birds, especially that "sleek dandy of the marshes," the red-winged blackbird, signify that spring is on the way, even though it is still winter on the calendar and the spring solstice is three weeks away.

At the end of February, a huge flock of blackbirds, mostly redwings interspersed with a few grackles, descended on my backyard, far from any marsh. They alighted in some tall ash trees, emanating a discordant and deafening din, and came down in noisy groups to feast on sunflower seeds in my bird feeders. The finches, juncos, cardinals, and other birds that had dined all winter in the yard took sudden flight at this invasion. The arrival of the blackbirds prompted me to wonder if redwings had also returned to the tidal wetlands.

The long winter seems to have imprisoned both my body and my soul. I am eager to get out and walk the edges of the marsh, to find some reassurance at Tivoli Bays, some glimpse of returning birds that will tell me that winter is dying and spring is on the way. And so on the first of March, I decide to drive up to

North Bay to find out.

With the early morning temperature at thirteen degrees, I wait until mid-afternoon for my excursion. The river at the Tivoli landing is filled with massive chunks of ice. Turning south, I drive slowly over the rough stones along the tracks for about a half mile and park alongside the old stone shed on the river's edge. To my dismay, the picturesque building, probably at one time a boat house for the estate on the bluff across the tracks, has been disfigured by bright blue graffiti since my last visit. The ground is littered with cigarette butts, beer cans, papers, and other debris. The once sturdy roof has collapsed into the shed, the result of the many years the shed has withstood the winds, snows, and other ravages of the elements. At the rear, an arched window, still intact, frames a view over the river to the tranquil mountains beyond.

Looking inside at the jumble of stone and broken concrete, I recall a March day a few years ago when I parked near the stone shed and looked in. To my horror, about two dozen skulls of decapitated deer, still with tatters of skin and fur hanging from them,

119

The old stone shed stands on the river's edge.

stared out at me. Poachers had evidently shot the deer, taken the meat and antlers, and disposed of the telltale remains in the isolated shed.

I shudder at the memory and think about death, as I did on that other day. The slaughter of the deer and the rude disposal of their remains made their death seem especially cruel and unnecessary. I am well aware that sudden death is common in the wild. Everything in these tidal wetlands, so rich in life, lives for awhile and than dies, and in dying, whether being eaten, being killed accidentally, or dying at the end of a life span, returns to earth and gives birth to new life. Death is part of the natural cycle of life, like the never-ending cycle of the tides. Wanton killing, however, is a disturbing event.

I turn sadly away from the shed and cross the railroad tracks to the east side. The northern boundary of Tivoli North Bay and the estuarine sanctuary lies at the foot of the bluff almost directly across the tracks from the crumbling stone shed.

The tide is very low. Great expanses of mud covered with dead brown stalks of sweet flag and broken or flattened cattail stalks are exposed. The old vegetation is beaten and bedraggled from the winter's depredations—the heavy snows, the constant onslaught of the tides, the icy winds. Dingy, broken bits of stems and seeds and leaves have been pushed by the tides into little indentations along the shore, forming an almost solid mat on the border of the marsh. Everywhere colors appear dull and sombre. Even the sun doesn't brighten the iron and ash grays, dirty tans, and tobacco browns of the still frozen marsh. A few wet streaks and small pools of water left by the ebbing tide are a muddy dark green color.

The brush bordering the railroad right-of-way along the edge of North Bay has been chopped down, probably by railroad crews. The debris is lying along the edge of the marsh in ragged unsightly heaps, adding to the general drab appearance of Tivoli North Bay today. My mind still burdened by thoughts of death, I begin to feel as though the marsh, too, is dead. The water is very still; there seems to be no tidal movement. Even the air is momentarily still; the March winds have stopped blowing. There are no bird sounds, no human sounds. Out in the river, the water too is quiet with only small ripples, no ship traffic, no visible currents, no movement of the ice floes.

Reaching the northernmost railroad bridge, I notice that the tide now seems to be coming in, flowing under the bridge into the large permanent pool at the inlet. The movement is marked by a few telltale leaves and twigs and other bits of debris floating marshward. I am reassured. The tides are still flowing in their never-ending cycle in the estuary and in and out of the bays. A sudden wind blows off the river. A gathering of geese takes off from the pool with much honking as I walk onto the bridge abutment projecting into the marsh. Several black ducks also take wing at my approach and fly out over the river. A single gull soars overhead.

Sitting on the bridge abutment, I am sheltered from the now sharp March wind. I listen and watch. The ice under the bridge is thin and transparent. Because the tide becomes more forceful as it narrows down on its passage under the bridge, the ice does not freeze solidly, as it does elsewhere in some inner reaches of the bay. The constant surge of the tide under the bridge pushes up thin jagged plates of ice. Rocked by the movement, they make a tinkling sound like breaking glass, punctuated by the percussive beats of large floes banging against the bridge abutment on the river side—a winter symphony created by ice and tide. In the distance, the honking of geese over the river adds another note to the marshland music.

A sharp-eyed muskrat suddenly peeks around the edge of the other bridge abutment across the inlet, but scoots quickly back into hiding when it sees me. Within the next ten minutes two Amtrak trains, one streaking north, the other south, rumble frighteningly across the bridge, drowning out the winter symphony. Three ducks explode into the air as the trains roar by. I wonder about the long-term impact of the constant rail traffic on geese and ducks, the shy muskrat, and other wetland wildlife. How do the noise and pollution affect them? Is it one of the factors in the gradual decline of some species?

The sun is descending lower in the west over the river. In spite of the cold wind, I decide to wait another half hour or so to capture on camera the momentary amber light of sunset on the marsh. At about five o'clock, the light suddenly turns to gold, and the marsh is illumined by a pre-sunset glow. The sweep of cattails, the gently waving plumes of the reeds, the shrubs on the edge of the wetland, the clumps of pale

The north end of North Bay lies directly under Sycamore Point.

The setting sun lights up foxtail grasses on the marsh's edge.

foxtail grass beween the railroad tracks and the marsh—all the muted winter colors are suffused with this radiant orange glow, while the blue of the sky seems more intense.

Precisely at 5:30, great waves of blackbirds begin to fly overhead from North Bay to the tall trees on Magdalen Island. Their hoarse calls fill the air. As the sun sinks slowly down ten minutes later, their tiny black shapes are silhouetted against the red cloud formations. Repeated groups fly toward the setting sun, seeking a safe roost for the night. I watch enchanted as the light fades, and still they fly.

I had expected to find a few early returnees from the south. Instead a tremendous flock of blackbirds has already arrived. These are probably not resident birds but a migrant flock on its way to some other wetland farther north. The resident redwings will return later in the month. As the sun sets, the marsh is alive with birds. While I fretted over the dull drab colors and the lack of movement and sound an hour ago, the blackbirds have been gathering and feeding somewhere in the cattails, waiting for the moment when they start their evening flight towards the safe roosting trees on the little island in the river. Although winter still presides over the wetlands in the beginning of March, the return of the blackbirds is the promise of spring.

According to ornithologists, the "blackbirds" of Europe, made familiar to many chidren by the old English nursery rhyme about "four and twenty blackbirds baked in a pie," were not really blackbirds, but a kind of European thrush. Although black, they were not related to the blackbirds of the New World. When English colonists came to this country and saw the countless blackbirds, they simply named them after the European birds without regard to scientific distinctions.

True blackbirds, like the red-winged blackbirds of Tivoli Bays, live only in the Western Hemisphere. "Not all birds classified as blackbirds are black, nor are all black birds classified as blackbirds," ornithologist Gordon Orians wrote.[1]

Blackbirds are members of the family Icteridae, which includes both black and highly colored species, among them red-winged blackbirds, grackles, orioles, bobolinks, yellow-headed blackbirds, meadowlarks, even the unloved cowbirds who lay their eggs in nests of other species and whose greedy offspring often cause the death of the rightful nestlings. In my ignorance, I initially thought that crows and ravens, the blackest of all black birds, were related to redwings and other blackbirds, but soon discovered that they are not even distant cousins.

Most familiar of all the blackbirds of North America and most widespread are the red-winged blackbirds. The jaunty fellows with the red and yellow shoulder patches can be found across North America in varied habitats—in salt and freshwater marshes, prairie potholes, upland meadows, wherever there are some water and certain types of vegetation in which to hide their nests. Marshes and swamps with cattails, reeds, sedges, and similar growths are their preferred breeding grounds.

The redwing's scientific name, *Agelaius phoenicius*, is a clue to its behavior and color. The first part comes from the Greek and refers to its social habit of belonging to a flock, while the second part derives from a Latin word for "purple-red."[2]

These winged messengers of spring returning to Tivoli North Bay are all males. By mid-March the old winter cattails, the dry stalks of purple loosestrife, and the other brown and tan vegetation that have survived the winter are dotted with male redwings, pecking at the cattail heads in search of insects. Little food is available in the late winter, and conditions are harsh, but the redwings seem oblivious as they seek to establish their territories in anticipation of the mating season. The smaller, less flamboyant females, streaked black and white with brown above, will arrive in two or three weeks.

A few days later, as I walk down Cruger Island Road after a warmer than usual March night, again searching for early signs of spring, I hear a single bell-like note off in the distance. It is followed by a brief pause, then four more loud silvery "peeps." The peepings are repeated, the first plaintive voice is followed by another, and in a few minutes a wild

Hundreds of returning blackbirds roost in a tree on Cruger Island Road.

chorus of shrill voices joins in and fills the early morning air. I am hearing the voice of the spring peeper, *Pseudacris crucifer*.

I know that when the first blackbirds return as winter draws to an end, they will be followed by the clear birdlike mating calls of this tiny treefrog. A combination of rain and daytime temperatures hovering between forty five and fifty degrees is usually needed to call them out of their winter hiding places. As early as the end of February or as late as April, they find their way to the nearest swamp, pond, or temporary pool for this annual rite. They are probably not in the tidal swamp bordering Cruger Island Road. The rising and falling tides would disturb their mating and egg laying, which will take place within a few weeks after the males begin to call. The unseen choristers are off in the distance, probably in a small marsh in an old pasture on the north side of Cruger Island Road. Their piercing voices can be heard at least a half-mile away.

I do not seek them out this morning. I recall exciting nighttime expeditions with young children to find this little creature with the loud voice. With flashlights in hand, we followed the sound when they were singing. As we approached the calls, they stopped abruptly. Waiting quietly until the singing resumed, we then walked softly while they were trilling. Sometimes, they ceased calling again, but the tiny amphibians were persistent and soon took up the fairy refrain. When we were close to their orchestra pit, we shone our flashlights around on the bushes and pale winter grasses and reed stems on the edge of the water. A light eventually fell on a gleaming white spot—the extended vocal sac of a singing male. Closer examination revealed a diminutive being. It was almost perfectly camouflaged by its muddy tan coloring except for its vocal sac, which was inflated like a little white balloon as it called. If we were lucky, we might capture a tiny singer. Holding it for a few moments, we discerned a dark brown cross on its back, the marking which gives it the second part of its scientific name, *crucifer*, meaning "cross-bearing."

What would the world be like if we could no longer hear the silvery notes of the spring peeper in the wetlands? Herpetologists and other observers of amphibian life have noted a gradual decline in the population

What if the bullfrog no longer bellows in spring? *Photographed in a Rhinebeck pond.*

of some species of frogs and toads in the United States. A general decline has also been noted worldwide. Studies are ongoing to determine the causes. Is it due to encroaching civilization and industrialization, with the accompanying pollution and loss of habitat, as in the case of the rare golden club in our area and other disappearing species? Are there other factors? I hope there will never be a time when the tinkling voices of the spring peepers, followed in succession, as spring proceeds, by the croaking calls of wood frogs, the trilling of toads, the bellowing of bullfrogs, will no longer be heard.

Continuing along the Cruger Island causeway, I make my way through a rough jumble of tide-tossed crumbly ice. Many old cattails are bent or broken. Some still stand erect; most of their frankfurter-shaped fruits, once trim and brown, are ragged and fluffed out with escaping seeds, like old men with massive heads of shaggy white hair. A tiny black-capped chickadee flits back and forth, seeking the cattail moth larvae hidden in the spikes. The chickadees have sustained themselves through the long winter on these larvae and any other insects and seeds they can find in the ice-bound wetlands and the forest. The returning red-wings also eat whatever food is available, existing on seeds, insects, and wild fruits still clinging to the vegetation.

By mid-March, the tidal swamp along Cruger Island causeway has assumed a different look from two weeks ago. The tidal creeks are open, with little ice remaining. On the afternoon of March 15, I find myself wading through large puddles left by a combination of melted snow and ice and the last high tide. In the marshy shallows, tips of new growth of the ubiquitous spatterdock are poking out of the water. Bordering the wetland, the bright yellow of the willow shrub and the blood-red stems of the red-osier dogwood are other signs of approaching spring. Pussy willows will soon follow.

Out on Cruger Island patches of snow remain in the forest. The trail is covered with a heavy layer of brown oak leaves that have not yet decomposed. Fallen leaves, twigs, and buds of maple, ash, and other trees, assisted by soil insects and the winter's heavy snows, are already decaying, returning nutrients to the soil. The edges of the trail are enlivened by bright green mosses and ferns, and colorful lichens are exposed on fallen logs.

A new chorus of bird sound floats down from the tree tops, the welcome voices of other birds which have returnd from their sojourn in the south. In my backyard a few days ago I saw a fox sparrow, large and rusty brown, searching for seeds on the ground with a characteristic hop-forward, scratch-backward movement; robins were digging in the moist ground, and a handsome flicker stopped by to garner some seeds at the shelf feeder. Expert birder Helen Manson Andrews, in a March column in the Taconic Newspapers, mentions woodcock, song sparrows, white-throated sparrows, bluebirds, and yellow-bellied sapsuckers also among the March returnees.[3] All of these species are known in the Tivoli Bays area.

On March 20, I return to the edge of North Bay along the railroad embankment south of Tivoli. The temperature is in the fifties. What will the wetlands be like today, just before the hour of the vernal equinox, scheduled for 10:02 tonight?

When I step out of the van alongside the old stone shed, a blast of wind from the river nearly knocks me over. Although it was windy when I left home, I am not prepared for the wild gusts. Charlie, who accompanied me on this marsh foray, elects to stay in the van after walking a few hundred feet in the stiff wind.

Shouldering my tripod and camera bag, I start south along the tracks. The wind pushes and shoves me, blowing fiercely from the north. The river, too, is wild, whipped into whitecaps. Large waves are beating against the shore. There is no sign of the ice floes which choked the estuary a few weeks ago. The

Tips of new growth of spatterdock in the tide swamp are a sign of spring.

current is flowing south, but I can't tell whether it is caused by the wind or the tide or both. When I reach the bridge, I can see that the tide is flooding out of the marsh on its journey back to the sea, aided by the north wind.

East of the railroad causeway, the marsh is a bit calmer than the river, but even these usually flat waters are deeply rippled, and waves move hypnotically along the outgoing tidal currents. The wind howls and moans around my ears, although there are no big trees for it to moan through. Strange phenomenon! The only other times I have heard the wind moan have been in forests; I always thought the sound was caused by wind blowing through tree branches. I feel as though I am on the edge of the ocean, with a storm wind and great waves crashing around me. When I tell Charlie later that it felt like being on the ocean, he confirms my description, saying that it reminds him of a storm on the North Atlantic, when he served as a merchant seaman on a freighter during World War II.

Despite the rough wind, the sky is a clear cloudless light blue. The water in the marsh is a deeper blue, while the river is almost black. At the bridge, I sit for a while on the concrete abutment, holding on to my tripod-mounted camera for fear it might be blown into the bay.

Walking back to the van, I watch a small flock of about a dozen Canada geese flying north over the marsh. They wheel and tack gracefully, flying back perhaps twenty-five to fifty feet for every fifty to seventy-five feet forward. The late sun shines on their white breasts each time they wheel back, creating a beautiful pattern against the blue sky. I wonder how a bird can withstand the blasts of wind that almost stop me in my tracks. No redwings or other small birds have ventured out. They stay sheltered in the cattails and loosestrife while the wind talks, moans, and roars off the river and across the wetlands. The spring equinox is now only a few hours away, but the wild wind has turned the spring-like day seemingly back into winter.

The last week of March remains chilly, despite the calendar that now says "Spring," but each day more redwings return to the marsh. The latest returnees are females, which continue to arrive well into the month of April. As mating begins, the little brown-streaked female sometimes exhibits an interesting behavior, taking an active part in the courtship. Thomas Proctor wrote in 1897 of the female: "And very amusing indeed it was to watch these comedians in sober brown, but in extemporized ruffs, puffs and puckers, pirouette, bow and posture, and thus quite out-do in airs and graces their blackcoated gallants."[4]

After mating, the nest is constructed entirely by the female, although the male sometimes engages in a little symbolic nest building. The female also does all the incubation of eggs and feeding of the young,

Grass stems are reflected in the marsh water.

with only an occasional tidbit being offered by the male.

One day, as we were discussing the red-winged blackbirds of Tivoli Bays, I remarked to my son that the flashy male seemed of little help in the propagation of his offspring, spending most of his time showing off his colors. Erik immmediately pointed out that the role of the male, first in selecting a territory that offered ample food, shelter, and good nesting sites, and then in defending it and the nest against other male blackbirds and predators, was extremely important in the perpetuation of the species and required a great expenditure of energy.

Along the edges of the marsh, tree buds are swelling, catkins are dangling from alder and birch, plump fuzzy pussy willows decorate the willows. The month of March is both the last month of the old year and the first month of the new year as winter fades and spring returns to the wetlands, connecting the circle of the seasons.

⊛ ⊛ ⊛

At the end of another March a few years later, I am resting contemplatively on the bridge abutment overlooking North Bay. When I arrived the tide was flowing silently under the railroad bridge and into the bay. As I watch, the water begins to flow outward. Bits of debris, broken cattail stalks, old brown leaves are carried under the bridge into the river. The never-ending tides have reversed and are ebbing out of the wetlands. They will surge southward down the Hudson estuary to the ocean, inevitably returning six hours later.

Changing tides—like the rhythms of my life. When I first began exploring and photographing the wetlands of Tivoli Bays I was seventy-two years old. Now I have passed my eighty-third birthday, and my life seems to be changing ever more rapidly. My husband and companion of fifty-one years, who in

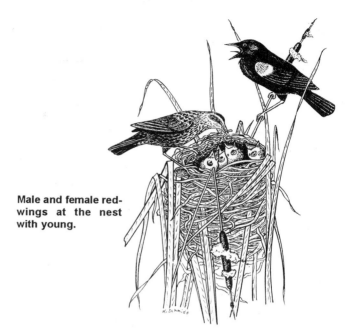

Male and female red-wings at the nest with young.

the early years of the Tivoli Bays project accompanied me on countless excursions, died four years ago. I have suffered a shattered kneecap and a loss of vision in my right eye in the past few years. Now I am not so surefooted or sharp-eyed as I was at seventy-two. It is becoming difficult to recognize birds, to clamber up and down over the raised bed of the railroad tracks, to traverse the tide-covered rocks and slithery mud along the Cruger Island causeway, to carry my heavy photo equipment on the trails.

I look across the river toward the purple gently-rounded Catskill Mountains, covered by a slight haze. They, too, are ever changing, changing in color with the seasons and the changing light, being slowly ground away bit by bit by the erosive forces of wind and rain, freezing and thawing, but still standing in all their beauty against the sky. After these thousands of years, they still guard the estuary and look down upon the tidal wetlands of Tivoli Bays.

The misty purple mountains stand guard over the estuary.

Visiting the marsh today to enjoy the beauty of the wetlands and the mountains as the red-winged blackbirds and spring return, to listen to the quiet, to relax in the peace and solitude of this near-wilderness, I feel renewed. I cannot regain the passing years, but as the ever-changing tides ebb and flow, I feel that I am in harmony with the earth rhythms, and once again I gain strength from them.

☙ ☙ ☙

Flow on, River! flow with the flood-tide,
*   and ebb with the ebb-tide!*
Frolic on, crested and scallop-edg'd waves!
Gorgeous clouds of the sunset! drench with
*   your splendor me, or the*
*   men and women generations after me!*

Walt Whitman

AFTERWORD

Are you ready to walk the trails or put your canoe into the marsh? I hope you will explore Tivoli Bays or other freshwater tidal wetlands and shores. These areas of the eastern U.S. are at the nexus of human impacts on the coastal environment through residential, commercial, industrial, and recreational activities.

Changing Tides is about a photographer discovering the Tivoli Bays, the most-studied wetland complex on the Hudson River. My own experience of Tivoli Bays is that of a conservation scientist, trying to understand how the parts fit together and how to protect and manage the whole in the long term. Because this book will be an introduction to the natural history of the Hudson for many readers, I will add some further thoughts about the science and conservation of the Tivoli Bays, and the rest of the Hudson's marsh landscape, chapter by chapter.

Cattails: Is the recent shift from cattails to purple loosestrife or common reed encouraged by sediment deposition on the marsh surface? By water pollution? By muskrat activity or its decline? Increase of reed and loosestrife change the insect community and the bird community of the marsh, although the effects are poorly understood. Invasive plants and their management are a subject of much debate among ecologists and land managers.

Golden Club: This most striking plant of the Hudson was recently added to the list of species rare enough to be monitored by the New York Natural Heritage Program. Golden club is largely restricted to areas of firm sediments in the lower to middle intertidal zone at a few locations in the Hudson, where it is nonetheless subject to overgrowth by taller marsh plants; it is even more rare inland. The basic ecology of this species–including pollination, establishment of seedlings, and impact of grazing animals–is a mystery.

Snapping Turtle: Only one species of reptile is common in the Hudson River–the snapping turtle. Yet this is also one of the world's most PCB-contaminated animals! What effects do PCBs and other pollutants have on the embryonic development, survival, and behavior of Hudson River snapping turtles? Why are other reptiles and amphibians rare in the Hudson?

Water-chestnut: This plant is arguably the worst weed of the estuary. In India it is cultivated for its protein-rich nut and also used medicinally. Northern European peoples have, since the Neolithic, eaten so much water-chestnut that it is endangered in some countries. Can we learn to use it?

Mummichog: The mummichog is the most abundant and typical fish of the freshwater tidal marshes, and virtually the only fish that swims into the higher parts of the marshes with the rising tide. This species seems to be a critical link in the marsh food web, yet no one has studied the mummichog diet, or consumption of mummichogs by other animals (fishes, turtles, birds, mammals), in the Hudson.

Closed Gentian: Apart from wildflowers and a few places to stand and look out over the marsh, most people ignore the shoreline. The backdrop for the closed gentian is a narrow zone that stretches from the level of average high tide just a few meters inland. This habitat supports a great diversity of plant life and intense animal activity.

Cruger Island: Many of the Hudson River islands, Cruger particularly, have been magnets for Native Americans, homes and industries of the 1800s, and recreation in the current century. What characteristics have made the islands hotspots of human activity, and how have people altered island ecology over the centuries?

Duck Blinds: Like islands, but on a smaller scale, duck blinds provide a dry spot in the wet marsh, a view, and access to food resources and water transport. Any raised surface in a wetland, be it a rock, log, muskrat lodge, or dump, is a place for animals and plants to get out of the water.

Overwintering: A freshwater tidal marsh is a harsh place in winter, and only a few birds and mammals remain active. Which fishes move into the deeper waters of the river and which burrow into the mud? Where are the insects that feed on flowers, leaves, and stems?

Bald Eagle: The reinhabitation of the Hudson River by bald eagles is wonderful. But how will the PCBs and other pollutants affect nesting eagles and their young?

Water Birds: Herring gull, ring-billed gull, double-crested cormorant, black-crowned night-heron, black tern, American coot, as well as northern harrier and sharp-tailed sparrow, migrate along the Hudson and breed both on the coast and inland (e.g. central New York, the Great Lakes, southeastern Canada). Why don't these birds nest along the Hudson at places like the Tivoli Bays? Is it habitat, pollution, human disturbance?

Red-winged Blackbird: The redwing is one of several birds that readily nest in purple loosestrife. Do redwings also eat some of the insects that loosestrife attracts to the marsh? Do redwings also nest in phragmites?

And where do you fit in? As a hiker, birder, fisher, farmer, hunter, painter, boater, trapper, lover, roadbuilder, teacher? How do your activities in, and outside of, the Tivoli Bays affect this ecosystem? Do you have a role in trail erosion or maintenance, disturbance of animals or their management, Hudson River pollution or its reduction, the safety of people who visit the marsh? Think about how you can reduce your impacts on, and contribute to the preservation of, special places like Tivoli Bays.

Here is one way you can help: Your observations of the flora, fauna, and environment at Tivoli Bays and elsewhere along the Hudson are of interest to scientists who watch and study the river. Please report your observations—especially anything new, different, or unusual—to Hudsonia Ltd., Bard College #217, P.O. Box 5000, Annandale NY 12504-5000; 914-758-7053; kiviat@bard.edu.

Erik Kiviat Ph.D.
Executive Director, Hudsonia Ltd.
Assoc. Prof. of Environmental Studies, Bard College

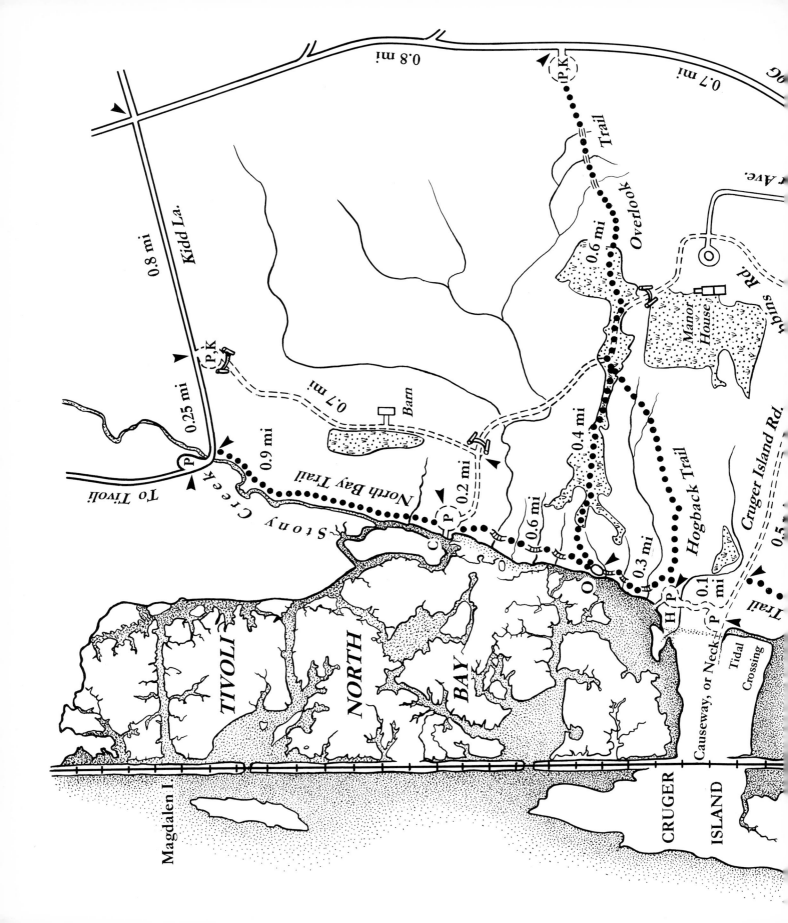

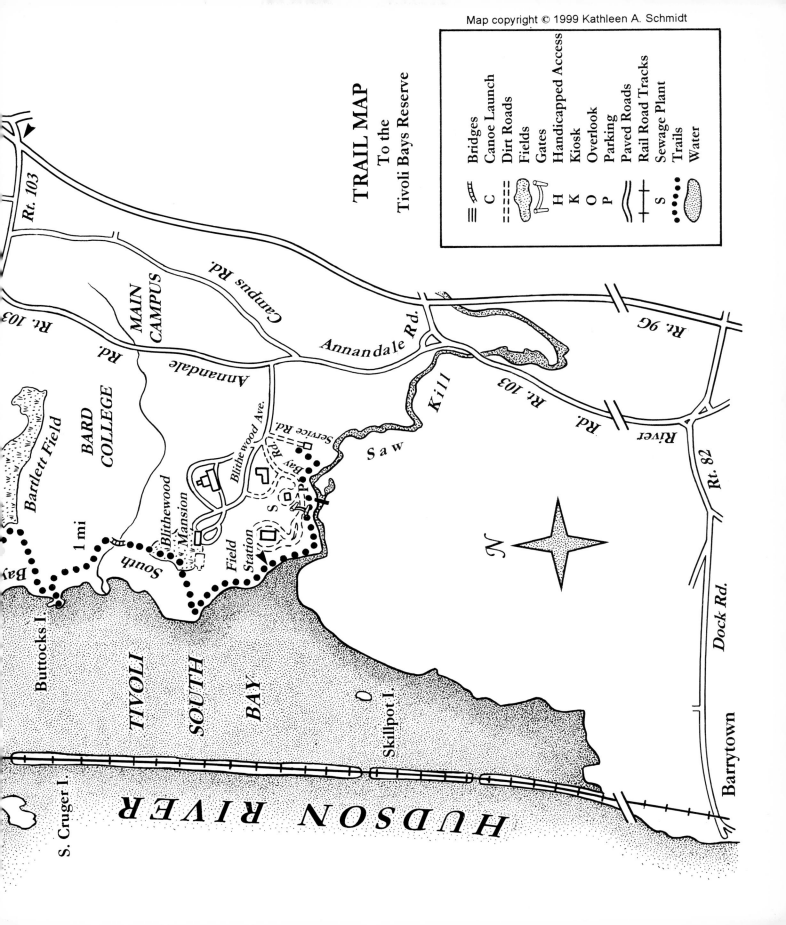

TRAIL MAP
To the
Tivoli Bays Reserve

Map copyright © 1999 Kathleen A. Schmidt

Bridges
C   Canoe Launch
Dirt Roads
Fields
Gates
H   Handicapped Access
K   Kiosk
O   Overlook
P   Parking
Paved Roads
Rail Road Tracks
S   Sewage Plant
Trails
Water

HUDSON RIVER

TIVOLI SOUTH BAY

S. Cruger I.

Skillpot I.

Buttocks I.

Bartlett Field

BARD COLLEGE

1 mi

Blithewood Mansion

Field Station

Blithewood Ave.

Service Rd.

Bay Rd.

South Bay

Saw Kill

Annandale Rd.

Campus Rd.

MAIN CAMPUS

Annandale Rd.

Rt. 103

Rt. 103

Rt. 103

Rt. 9G

River Rd.

Rt. 82

Dock Rd.

Barrytown

N

USER'S GUIDE to the TIVOLI BAYS RESERVE

Tivoli Bays, a component of the Hudson River National Estuarine Research Reserve, is located in northern Dutchess County in the Town of Red Hook, New York. Its 1700 acres are open from dawn to dusk for a variety of uses including hiking, canoeing, and nature study. The area also includes the Tivoli Bays Wildlife Management Area, which is hunted and trapped in season. Research and education activities are by permit. Rules and regulations apply. Printed materials and tide charts are available from the Research Reserve's office at (914)758-7010.

I. Trails and Trail Heads

North Bay Trail is a mile-long path from Kidd Lane to the Cruger Island Road parking area. It follows Stony Creek and the shore line of Tivoli North Bay past tidal wetlands, the Stony Creek canoe landing, and the North Bay overlook, to the Cruger Island Road parking circle. The north end of the trail can be picked up by parking in a small lot at the hard right turn in Kidd Lane, 0.75 miles from Route 9G, and walking east up Kidd Lane a short distance to the trail head on the right. The south end of the trail is reached via Dutchess County Road 103 and down Cruger Island Road 0.75 miles to a hard right turn to a parking circle. The trail can also be picked up at the Stony Creek canoe launch.

Overlook Trail is a 1.1 mile path from Route 9G parking area through rolling woods and fields to an overlook that offers superb views of Tivoli North Bay and the Catskills. The North Bay Trail intersects with the Overlook Trail at the overlook.

Hogback Trail is a 0.5 mile climb from the Cruger Island Road parking circle through woods to the Overlook Trail.

Saw Kill Trail is a 0.3 mile ramble beginning at Bard's water treatment plant and ending at the Ecology Field Station on Tivoli South Bay, headquarters for Hudsonia Ltd. and NYSDEC's Hudson River NERR. The water plant is reached by a dirt road running south from the intersection of Bay and Blithewood Roads. The trail passes a small waterfall and plunge pool, a concrete dam and millpond, and a lower waterfall that is one of the most exciting features of the Bard campus.

South Bay Trail is a 0.25 mile stroll from the Ecology Field Station to Blithewood Mansion, then another 0.75 miles to Cruger Island Road. The trail runs atop a bluff, offering fine views of Tivoli South Bay. You can find the beginning of the trail by following the Saw Kill trail or by walking Bay Road from its intersection with Blithewood Road to the field station.

II. Canoe/Kayak Access

Paddlers can reach Tivoli North and South Bays and Magdalen and Cruger Islands by launching at the Village of Tivoli riverfront (western end of Dutchess County Road 78) and paddling south about 1 mile. From that point the bays can be reached by paddling under either of two railroad bridges. Warning: Submerged pilings under these bridges pose potential hazard. Swift currents in either direction occur under these bridges at maximum flood or ebb currents.

Paddlers may put in directly to the sheltered backwaters of Tivoli North Bay at the Stony Creek canoe launch, via the Kidd Lane entrance, 0.5 miles from Route 9G. Once on state lands, bear right at a fork in the road (0.7 miles) and proceed another 0.25 miles to a turnaround, where one may park. The floating dock is a short walk down a small hill.

Paddle wisely. Carry proper safety equipment. Know the day's weather forecast and its tides. Tide charts are available from HRNERR. Daily tides often are posted in local papers. Bring protection from the elements.

III. Handicapped Facilites

The network of internal roads in the Tivoli Bays Wildlife Management Area offers fine opportunities for observing wildlife from the convenience of one's vehicle. The parking circle just off Cruger Island Road provides access to the North Bay viewing platform. A 150' hard-surface walkway leads to this at-grade platform affording panoramic views of Tivoli North Bay and the Catskills. This is also an excellent birding area.

IV. Directions

A. *From Ulster County (Kingston)*: Go east on Route 199 across Kingston-Rhinecliff Bridge and continue 1.3 miles to Route 9G. Turn left and travel (north) 4.5 miles to Route 9G parking area or 5.3 miles to Kidd Lane. Turn left onto Kidd Lane and travel 0.5 miles to the Kidd Lane entrance to the Research Reserve at the brown and yellow NYSDEC sign on the left.

For other entrances to the Research Reserve and trail heads, refer to the trail map on pages 132-133 and/or call the HRNERR at 914-758-7010 for directions.

B. *From Orange and Rockland Counties*: Travel north on the NYS Thruway to exit 19 (Kingston). Turn right onto traffic circle then right again; follow signs to Route 199 east and the Kingston-Rhinecliff Bridge. Then refer to directions from Ulster County above (A).

C. *From southern Dutchess, Putnam, and Westchester Counties*: Travel north on Route 9 through Rhinebeck, then turn left (north) onto Route 9G at traffic light at the intersection of Routes 9 and 9G. Drive 5.8 miles to Route 9G parking area or continue an additional 0.8 miles to Kidd Lane. Turn left onto Kidd Lane and travel 0.5 miles to the Kidd Lane entrance to the Research Reserve at the brown and yellow NYSDEC sign on the left.

Or travel Taconic Parkway to Route 199 exit for Pine Plains/Red Hook, then Route 199 west 9.2 miles to Route 9G. Turn right (north) and travel 2.6 miles to Route 9G parking area or an additional 0.8 miles to Kidd Lane.

D. *From Columbia County and northern Dutchess*: Follow signs to Rip Van Winkle Bridge but turn onto Route 9G south before crossing bridge. Travel on Route 9G 13.5 miles to Kidd Lane. Then refer to directions from southern Dutchess above (C) for Kidd Lane entrance.

Or take Taconic Parkway south to Route 199 exit for Pine Plains/Red Hook; then refer to directions from Taconic Parkway above (C).

E. *From Greene County and beyond*: Take Route 23 east and cross the Rip Van Winkle Bridge. Turn left (south) onto Route 9G. Then refer to directions from Columbia County and northern Dutchess above (D).

Dennis Mildner
Education Coordinator, HRNERR

NOTES

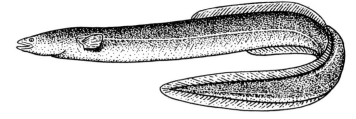

Preface

1. Joseph Wook Krutch. *The Desert Year*, (New York: Viking Compass Edition, The Vikng Press, 1963).

Chapter 1 - April: Cattails and Catskills

1. Kenneth Grahame. *Wind in the Willows*, (New York: Holt, Rinehart, and Winston, 1980).
2. See Chapter 4 - "July: Water Chestnuts in My Sneakers," for more information about Tivoli South Bay.
3. State law prohibits collecting plants or animals on state land.

Chapter 2 - May: In Pursuit of the Golden Club

1. See Chapter 7 - "October: The Autumn Island," for additional description of the Cruger Island causeway.
2. Henry David Thoreau. *Journal*, March 10, 1859.
3. Euell Gibbons. *Stalking the Healthful Herbs*, (New York: Field Guide Edition, David McKay Co., 1970).
4. Brian Swift. "Avian Breeding Habitats in Hudson River Tidal Marshes," (Albany, NY: New York State Department of Environmental Conservation, 1989).
5. Erik Kiviat. "Golden Club, A Threatened Plant in the Tidal Hudson," (Fourth Symposium for the Hudson River Ecology, Hudson River Environmental Society, 1976).
6. Steven Clements and Richard Mitchell. "Heartleaf Plantain - Kingroot," (Albany, NY: Newsletter of the New York Flora Association, New York State Museum Institute, Vol. 2, No. 2, July 1991).

Chapter 3 - June: Consider the Turtle

1. Henry David Thoreau. *Journal*, August 22, 1856
2. When biologist Wilfred T. Neill conducted his experiment, he concluded that "it seems doubtful that even the largest alligator snapper could bite through a broomstick." The experiment was described in *The Illustrated Encyclopedia of Animal Life*, Frederick Drimmer, Editor-in-Chief (New York: *Animal Kingdom*, Vol.11, Greystone Press, 1952).
3. Ward Stone, Erik Kiviat, and Stanley A. Butke. "Toxicants in Snapping Turtles," (New York Fish and Game Journal, Vol.2l, No.1, January 1990).
4. Donald C. Buso. Unpublished data.

Chapter 4 - July: Water Chestnuts in My Sneakers

1. Robert E. Schmidt and Erik Kiviat. "Communities of Larval and Juvenile Fish Associated with Water-Chestnut, Watermilfoil, and Water Celery in the Tivoli Bays of the Hudson River," (Annandale, NY: Unpublished research for the Hudson River Foundation, Hudsonia, Ltd., February 1988).
2. Erik Kiviat. "Tangled Locks: The Purple Loosestrife Invasion and Biological Diversity," (Annandale, NY: *Annandale*, Bard College, Fall 1995).
3. Ibid.
4. Albany, NY: *New York State Conservationist*, NYSDEC, August 1994.
5. K. E. Adams. "Prehistoric Reedgrass 'Cigarettes' with Tobacco Content, A Case Study from Red Bow Cliff Dwelling, Arizona," (*Journal of Ethnobiology*, Winter 1996).
6. John Bull. *Birds of New York State*, (Ithaca, NY and London: Comstock Publishing Associates, Cornell University Press, 1974. Reissued 1985).

Chapter 5 - August: Mummichogs, Monsters, and Dragons of the Air

1. This illustration of a dragonfly nymph was drawn from a specimen in a Hudson Valley pond.
2. C. Lavett Smith. *The Inland Fishes of New York State*, (Albany NY: NYSDEC, 1985).
3. Ibid.
4. Erik Kiviat. "Muskrat, Manager of the Marsh," (Annandale, NY: *News from Hudsonia*, Hudsonia Ltd., Vol.10, No. 3, 1994).

Chapter 6 - September: Where the Closed Gentian Blooms

1. Henry David Thoreau. *Walden*, (New York: Brooks Atkinson, Editor, *The Modern Library*, Random House, 1950).
2. See Trail Map and User's Guide, Appendix, pp. 132-35.
3. Ephraim Porter Felt. *Plant Galls and Gall Makers*, (New York: Facsimile of the 1940 Edition, Hafner Press, 1965).
4. John H. Bland. *Forests of Lilliput, The Realm of Mosses and Lichens*, (Englewood Cliffs, NJ: Prentice-Hall, 1971).
5. Small bridges are now being constructed by the NYSDEC across the ravines and intermittent streams, making this spectacular trail more accessible.

Chapter 7 - October: The Autumn Island

1. The names utilized today, "Cruger Island" and "Magdalen Island," are as they appear on the U.S. Geological Survey Map, Saugerties Quadrangle, NY, 1963.
2. William A. Ritchie. *An Introduction to Hudson Valley Prehistory*, (Albany, NY: New York State Museum and Science Service, Bulletin No. 367, University of State of New York, 1958).
3. Patricia Edwards Clyne. "Maya on the Hudson," (Poughkeepsie, NY: *Hudson Valley Magazine*, November 1984).
4. Hal Hillman. "Cruger's Island, History and Occupation," (Student research paper, Hudson Valley Studies, Bard College, 1983).
5. Euphemia Van Rensselaer Wyatt, a Cruger relative, in a memoir entitled "New York City Is On The Hudson" c. 1971, described Cruger Island, the house, and cousin Cornelia. Mrs. Wyatt spent many summers in Barrytown and "visited Cruger's Island every Friday afternoon."
6. Donna Matthews, granddaughter of William H. Matthews, who managed Ward Manor starting in 1926, shared with me a fascinating scrapbook kept by Mr. Matthews during his years at Ward Manor. It is illustrated with old photographs and many handwritten descriptions of activities of the enterprise.
7. Personal conversation on February 16, 1991 with a long-time resident of the area, who wished to remain anonymous.
8. This engraving of Cruger Island on rice paper appeared in the *Atlantic Coast Pilot, South Coast of Long Island, New York Bay, and Hudson River* (Washington, D.C.: Govt Printing Office, 1890).
9. A detailed account of this secret demonstration was related to me in personal conversation with John Carbary, a lifelong resident of Rhinebeck, on November 13 and 14, 1997.
10. A sign on Cruger Island Road, just past the sharp right turn leading to the parking lot and North Bay viewing platform, warns that only authorized vehicles are permitted beyond this point. The causeway beyond is tidal and often covered with high water.
11. Carbary related that an elderly friend, Freeman Cole, who worked with Delano Roosevelt, told him about the windmill. Freeman, who died at age 93, was familiar with Cruger Island in the 1800s. Carbary saw the remains of the greenhouse about twenty-two years ago when he last visited the island.
12. Herbert L. Edlin. *The Tree Key*, (London: Frederick Warne Ltd., 1978).

Chapter 8 - November: Duck Blinds and Deer Hunters

1. Erik Kiviat. "Hudson River East Bank Natural Areas, Clermont to Norrie," (Arlington, VA: The Nature Conservancy, 1978).
2. "Science Times," *New York Times*, February 9, 1988.
3. "Science Times," *New York Times*, November 11, 1994.
4. Caitlin Matthews. *The Celtic Book of Days*, (Rochester, Vermont: Destiny Books, 1995).

Chapter 9 - December: Where Have All the Creatures Gone

1. Matthews. *The Celtic Book of Days*.
2. The moon is at perigee when it is closest to the earth and its gravitational pull is strongest. See Chapter 1, p. 2 & 3, for additional explanation of tidal terminology.
3. Les Line. "Total Recall," (Virginia: *National Wildlife*, February-March 1998).
4. Dennis Chastain. "Come Winter," (Columbia, SC: *South Carolina Wildlife*, November-December, 1990).
5. See Chapter 5, p. 48, for more information on dragonfly nymphs.
6. Jeffrey K. Barnes. "The Ladybug That Left Home," (Albany, NY: *New York State Conservationist*, NYSDEC, October, 1997).

Chapter 10 - January: The Time of Cold and Ice

1. Matthews. *The Celtic Book of Days*.
2. Erik Kiviat. *Mills and Minnows, A Walk Down the Saw Kill*, (Annandale, NY: Hudsonia Ltd., 1986).
3. Henry David Thoreau. *Journal*, Jan. 21, 1853.
4. *New York Times*, Feb. 13, 1998
5. John Bull. *Birds of New York*, (Ithaca, NY: Comstock Publishing Associates, Cornell University Press, 1974, 1985).
6. Art Wolfe and Julio de la Torre. *Owls, Their Life and Behavior*, (New York: Crown Publishing Company, 1990).
7. Edward A. Armstrong. *The Folklore of Birds*, (London: Collins, 1958).
8. John Burroughs. *A Year in the Fields*, (Boston: Houghton Mifflin Company, 1896).
9. Angus Cameron and Peter Parnall. *The Nightwatchers*, (New York: Four Winds Press, 1972).

Chapter 11- February: Winter Wanderings

1. Roger Tory Peterson. *A Field Guide to the Birds East of the Rockies*, (Boston: Houghton Mifflin Co., 1980).
2. *Another Book for Old Bird Watchers, But Not Too Old*, (Lincoln, MA: Sawtells of Somerset, 1972).
3. Hal Borland. *Beyond Your Doorstep*, (New York: Alfred A. Knopf, 1962).
4. Claus Murie. *Field Guide to Animal Tracks*, (Boston: Houghton Mifflin Company, 1954).

Chapter 12- March: Return of the Blackbirds

1. Gordon Orions. *Blackbirds of the Americas*, (Seattle and London: University of Washington Press, 1985).
2. Robert W. Nero. *Redwings*, (Washington, D.C.: Smithsonian Institution Press, 1984).
3. Helen Manson Andrews. "Birding," (Millbrook, N.Y.: "Weekend," Taconic Newspapers, March 9, 1995).
4. Thomas Proctor's comments on female redwings' courtship behavior are quoted by Arthur Cleveland Bent in *Life Histories of North American Blackbirds, Orioles, Tanagers, and Allies*, (New York: Dover Publications, Inc., 1965).

SUGGESTED READING

Boyle, Robert H. *The Hudson River; A Natural and Unnatural History.* Expanded edition. New York: W.W. Norton 1979.

Errington, Paul L. *Of Men and Marshes.* Ames: Iowa State University Press 1957.

Kiviat, Erik. "A Fresh-Water Tidal Marsh on the Hudson, Tivoli North Bay." Paper 14 in Third Symposium on Hudson River Ecology. Bronx, NY: Hudson River Environmental Society 1974.

Kiviat, Erik and Gretchen Stevens. In Preparation. *Biodiversity Assessment Manual for the Hudson River Corridor.* New York State Department of Environmental Conservation.

Limburg, Karin, M. A. Moran, and W. H. McDowell. *The Hudson River Ecosystem.* New York: Springer-Verlag 1986.

Mildner, Dennis. *Birds of the Hudson River National Estuarine Research Reserve.* Annandale, NY: Hudson River National Estuarine Research Reserve 1994.

Mildner, Dennis. *Hudson River Field Guide to Plants of Freshwater Tidal Wetlands.* Illustrated by L.B. McCloskey. Albany, NY: New York State Department of Environmental Conservation (Available from Hudson River National Estuarine Research Reserve.) 1998.

Niering, William A. *Wetlands of North America.* Photography by B. Littlehales. Charlottesville, VA: Thomasson-Grant 1991.

Odum, William T., T. J. Smith III, and C. McIvor. *The Ecology of Tidal Freshwater Marshes of the United States East Coast: A Community Profile.* U.S. Fish and Wildlife Service, FWS/OBS-83/17, 1984.

Stanne, Steve. and R. Panetta, eds. *A Hudson River Primer.* Poughkeepsie, NY: Hudson River Sloop Clearwater, 1994.

Tiner, Ralph W., Jr. *Field Guide to Costal Wetland Plants of the Northeastern United States.* Amherst: University of Massachusetts Press 1987.

Tiner, Ralph W., Jr. *Field Guide to Nontidal Wetland Identification.* Annapolis: Maryland Department of Natural Resources 1988.

SCIENTIFIC NAMES of PLANTS and ANIMALS

Plants

Acanthopanax, five leaf	*Acanthopanax sieboldianus*
Apple, common	*Malus pumila*
Arrowhead, broadleaf	*Sagittaria latifolia*
Arum, arrow	*Peltandra virginica*
Ash	*Fraxinus*
Aster	*Aster*
Basswood	*Tilia americana*
Beech, American	*Fagus grandifolia*
Beggar-ticks	*Bidens*
Birch, black	*Betula lenta*
Bittersweet, Oriental	*Celastrus orbiculata*
Blue-eyed grass	*Sisyrinchium*
Boneset, white	*Eupatorium perfoliatum*
Buckthorn, common	*Rhamnus cathartica*
Bugloss, viper's	*Echium vulgare*
Bulrush	*Scirpus*
Bur-marigold	*Bidens*
Burdock	*Arctium*
Butter-and-eggs	*Linaria vulgaris*
Buttercup	*Ranunculus*
Buttonbush	*Cephalanthus occidentalis*
Cardinal flower	*Lobelia cardinalis*
Cattail, broadleaf	*Typha latifolia*
Cattail, narrowleaf	*Typha angustifolia*
Cedar, red	*Juniperus virginiana*
Cherry, bird	*Prunus avium*
Cherry, black	*Prunus serotina*
Coneflower, green-headed	*Rudbeckia laciniata*
Coontail	*Ceratophyllum demersum*
Creeper, Virginia	*Parthenocissus*
Daisy, ox-eye	*Leucanthemum vulgare*
Dandelion, common	*Taraxacum officinale*
Day-lily, orange	*Hemerocallis fulva*
Dogwood, red-osier	*Cornus sericea*
Dogwood, silky	*Cornus amomum*
Duckweed	Lemnaceae
Evening primrose	*Oenothera biennis*
False-indigo	*Amorpha fruticosa*
Figwort	*Scrophularia*
Flag, blue	*Iris versicolor*
Forsythia	*Forsythia*
Garlic-mustard	*Alliaria petiolata*
Gentian, closed	*Gentiana andrewsii*
Gentian, fringed	*Gentiana crinita*
Geranium, wild	*Geranium maculatum*
Golden club	*Orontium aquaticum*
Goldenrod	*Solidago*
Grape, wild	*Vitis*
Grass, foxtail	*Setaria*
Grass, redhead	*Potamogeton perfoliatus*
Ground-ivy	*Glechoma hederacea*
Hedge bindweed	*Calystegia sepium*
Hemlock	*Tsuga canadensis*
Hepatica, blunt-lobed	*Hepatica nobilis* var. *obtusa*
Hickory	*Carya*
Honeysuckle, Bell's	*Lonicera* x *bella*
Hornbeam, hop	*Ostrya virginiana*
Horsetail	*Equisetum*
Iris, yellow	*Iris pseudacorus*
Jack-in-the-pulpit	*Arisaema triphyllum* s.l.
Jewelweed	*Impatiens capensis*
Joe-Pye weed	*Eupatorium*
Lily, Canada	*Lilium canadense*
Loosestrife, purple	*Lythrum salicaria*
Mallow, swamp rose-	*Hibiscus moscheutos*
Maple, red	*Acer rubrum*
Maple, sugar	*Acer saccharum*
Marsh marigold	*Caltha palustris*
Micranthemum, Nuttall's	*Micranthemum micranthemoides*
Milkweed, swamp	*Asclepias incarnata*
Mullein	*Verbascum thapsus*
Ninebark	*Physocarpus opulifolius*
Oak, black	*Quercus velutina*
Oak, northern red	*Quercus rubra* var. *borealis*
Oak, white	*Quercus alba*
Peach	*Prunus persica*
Pear	*Pyrus communis*
Periwinkle, common	*Vinca minor*
Pickerelweed	*Pontederia cordata*
Plantain, heartleaf	*Plantago cordata*
Poison-ivy	*Toxicodendron radicans*
Queen Anne's lace	*Daucus carota*
Reed, common	*Phragmites australis*
Rice, wild	*Zizania aquatica*
Rose, swamp	*Rosa palustris*
Sassafras	*Sassafras albidum*
Shadbush	*Amelanchier*
Skunk cabbage	*Symplocarpus foetidus*
Smartweed	*Polygonum*
Sneezeweed	*Helenium autumnale*
Spatterdock	*Nuphar advena*
Spicebush	*Lindera benzoin*
Spikerush, ovate	*Eleocharis ovata*
Sunflower	*Helianthus*
Sweet-gum	*Liquidambar styraciflua*
Sweetflag	*Acorus*
Sycamore, American	*Platanus occidentalis*
Toadflax, oldfield	*Linaria canadensis*
Tree-of-heaven	*Ailanthus altissima*
Trillium, red	*Trillium erectum*
Tulip-tree	*Liriodendron tulipifera*
Viburnum, maple-leaf	*Viburnum acerifolium*
Violet	*Viola*
Virgins-bower	*Clematis virginiana*
Water-chestnut	*Trapa natans*
Watermilfoil, Eurasian	*Myriophyllum spicatum*
Wild-celery	*Vallisneria americana*
Willow, pussy	*Salix discolor*
Witch-hazel	*Hamamelis virginiana*

Animals

Alewife	*Alosa pseudoharengus*	Fox, gray	*Urocyon cinereoargenteus*
Backswimmers	Notonectidae	Fox, red	*Vulpes vulpes*
Bass, striped	*Morone saxatilis*	Frog, wood	*Rana sylvatica*
Bat, big brown	*Eptesicus fuscus*	Goldfinch, American	*Carduelis tristis*
Bat, little brown	*Myotis lucifugus*	Goldfish	*Carassius auratus*
Beaver	*Castor canadensis*	Goose, Canada	*Branta canadensis*
Beetle, bark	Scolytidae	Grackle, common	*Quiscalus quiscula*
Beetle, diving	Dytiscidae	Grasshopper, meadow	*Conocephalus*
Beetle, Japanese	*Popillia japonica*	Grouse, ruffed	*Bonasa umbellus*
Beetle, water-lily leaf	*Galerucella nymphaeae*	Gull, greater black-backed	*Larus marinus*
Beetle, whirligig	Gyrinidae	Gull, herring	*Larus argentatus*
Bee, honey	*Apis mellifera*	Gull, ring-billed	*Larus delawarensis*
Bittern, American	*Botaurus lentiginosus*	Harrier, northern	*Circus cyaneus*
Bittern, least	*Ixobrychus exilis*	Hawk, Cooper's	*Accipiter cooperii*
Blackbird, red-winged	*Agelaius phoeniceus*	Hawk, red-tailed	*Buteo jamaicensis*
Bluebird, eastern	*Sialia sialis*	Heron, great blue	*Ardea herodias*
Bluegill	*Lepomis macrochirus*	Herring, blueback	*Alosa aestivalis*
Bluet	*Enallagma*	Hornet, bald faced	*Dolichovestula maculata*
Boatman, water	Corixidae	Hoverfly	Syrphidae
Bobcat	*Felis rufus*	Insect, reed scale	*Chaetococcus phragmitidis*
Bufflehead	*Bucephala albeola*	Jay, blue	*Cyanocitta cristata*
Bug, June	*Phyllophaga*	Junco, dark-eyed	*Junco hyemalis*
Bug, water-measurer	Hydrometridae	Kestrel, American	*Falco sparverius*
Bullfrog	*Rana catesbeiana*	Killifish, banded	*Fundulus diaphanus*
Bullhead, brown	*Ictalurus nebulosus*	Kingbird, eastern	*Tyrannus tyrannus*
Butterfly, black swallowtail	*Papilio polyxenes*	Kingfisher, belted	*Ceryle alcyon*
Butterfly, monarch	*Danaus plexippus*	Kinglet, golden-crowned	*Regulus satrapa*
Caddisfly or caddisworm	Trichoptera	Ladybeetle, Asian	*Harmonia axyridis*
Canvasback	*Aythya valisineria*	Ladybeetle, nine-spotted	*Cocinella novemnotata*
Carp, common	*Cyprinus carpio*	Ladybeetle, twelve-spotted	*Coleomegilla maculata*
Catbird, gray	*Dumetella carolinensis*	Mallard	*Anas platyrhynchos*
Catfish, white	*Ictalurus catus*	Mayfly	Ephemeroptera
Chickadee, black-capped	*Parus atricapillus*	Meadowlark, eastern	*Sturnella neglecta*
Chipmunk, eastern	*Tamias striatus*	Merganser, common	*Mergus merganser*
Cicada	Cicadidae	Mink	*Mustela vison*
Clubtail	*Gomphus*	Mole, starnose	*Condylura cristata*
Cormorant, double-crested	*Phalacrocorax auritus*	Moorhen, common	*Gallinula chloropus*
Cottontail, eastern	*Sylvilagus floridanus*	Moth, cattail	*Lymnaecia phragmitella*
Cowbird, brown-headed	*Molothrus ater*	Moth, promethea	*Callosamia promethea*
Coyote, eastern	*Canis latrans* var.	Mouse, white-footed	*Peromyscus leucopus*
Crayfish	Decapoda	Mummichog	*Fundulus heteroclitus*
Crow, American	*Corvus brachyrhynchos*	Muskrat	*Ondatra zibethicus*
Darner, green	*Anax junius*	Nuthatch, white-breasted	*Sitta carolinensis*
Darter, tessellated	*Etheostoma olmstedi*	Opossum, Virginia	*Didelphis marsupialis*
Deer, white-tailed	*Odocoileus virginianus*	Oriole, northern	*Icterus galbula*
Duck, black	*Anas rubripes*	Osprey	*Pandion haliaetus*
Duck, wood	*Aix sponsa*	Owl, barred	*Strix varia*
Eagle, bald	*Haliaeetus leucocephalus*	Owl, great horned	*Bubo virginianus*
Eel, American	*Anguilla rostrata*	Owl, long-eared	*Asio otus*
Egret, great	*Egretta alba*	Owl, northern saw-whet	*Aegolius acadicus*
Egret, snowy	*Egretta thula*	Owl, snowy	*Nyctea scandiaca*
Falcon, peregrine	*Falco peregrinus*	Peeper, spring	*Hyla crucifer*
Finch, purple	*Carpodacus purpureus*	Perch, white	*Morone americana*
Flea, water	*Daphnia*	Pheasant, ring-necked	*Phasianus colchicus*
Flicker, northern	*Colaptes auratus*	Phoebe, eastern	*Sayornis phoebe*
Flycatcher, willow	*Empidonax traillii*	Pintail, northern	*Anas acuta*

Pirate, blue	*Pachydiplax longipennis*
Pumpkinseed	*Lepomis gibbosus*
Raccoon	*Procyon lotor*
Rail, king	*Rallus elegans*
Rail, Virginia	*Rallus limicola*
Rat, Norway	*Rattus norvegicus*
Raven, northern	*Corvus corax*
Redhead (duck)	*Aythya americana*
Redstart, American	*Setophaga ruticilla*
Robin, American	*Turdus migratorius*
Sapsucker, yellow-bellied	*Sphyrapicus varius*
Screech-owl, eastern	*Otus asio*
Shad, American	*Alosa sapidissima*
Shiner, spottail	*Notropis hudsonius*
Shoveler, northern	*Anas clypeata*
Shrew, northern shorttail	*Blarina brevicauda*
Skunk, striped	*Mephitis mephitis*
Snake, common garter	*Thamnophis sirtalis*
Sora	*Porzana carolina*
Sparrow, song	*Melospiza melodia*
Sparrow, swamp	*Melospiza georgiana*
Sparrow, white-crowned	*Zonotrichia leucophrys*
Sparrow, white-throated	*Zonotrichia albicollis*
Squirrel, gray	*Sciurus carolinensis*
Squirrel, red	*Tamiasciurus hudsonicus*
Starling, European	*Sturnus vulgaris*
Swallow, barn	*Hirundo rustica*
Swallow, tree	*Tachycineta bicolor*
Swan, mute	*Cygnus olor*
Swan, trumpeter	*Cygnus buccinator*

Swan, tundra	*Cygnus columbianus*
Teal, blue-winged	*Anas discors*
Teal, green-winged	*Anas crecca*
Terrapin, diamondback	*Malaclemys terrapin*
Thrush, hermit	*Catharus guttatus*
Thrush, wood	*Hylocichla mustelina*
Titmouse, tufted	*Parus bicolor*
Toad, American	*Bufo americanus*
Towhee, rufous-sided	*Pipilo erythrophthalmus*
Treefrog, gray	*Hyla versicolor*
Turkey, wild	*Meleagris gallopavo*
Turtle, map	*Graptemys geographica*
Turtle, painted	*Chrysemys picta*
Turtle, snapping	*Chelydra serpentina*
Turtle, wood	*Clemmys insculpta*
Vireo, red-eyed	*Vireo olivaceus*
Vireo, white-eyed	*Vireo gilvus*
Vole, meadow	*Microtus pennsylvanicus*
Warbler, yellow	*Dendroica petechia*
Weasel, longtail	*Mustela frenata*
Weasel, short-tailed	*Mustela erminea*
Wolf, timber	*Canis lupus*
Woodchuck	*Marmota monax*
Woodcock, American	*Scolopax minor*
Woodpecker, downy	*Picoides pubescens*
Woodpecker, hairy	*Picoides villosus*
Woodpecker, pileated	*Dryocopus pileatus*
Wren, marsh	*Cistothorus palustris*
Yellowthroat, common	*Geothlypis trichas*

Esther Kiviat

Writer
photographer
environmental educator

Born in Michigan, she has lived most of her eighty-plus years in the mid-Hudson Valley. She taught herself photography as an aid to successive careers, including newspaper columnist, publicist, teacher of all ages from nursery school through college, owner-director of a nature camp, and environmental educator.

In the last two decades she has devoted herself full-time to writing and photography, based on her lifelong interest in the natural environment. Her award-winning photographs have been widely exhibited, and along with her writings have appeared in local, regional, and national publications.

Her photography, she says, is "not just a factual rendition of a landscape, a flower, or a living creature, but my deep emotional response to nature–its beauty, its wildness, its fragility as well as its strength, and most of all its interconnectedness, of which we are an integral part."

The Tivoli Bays photographs were taken with a medium-format Hasselblad, supplemented by 35mm Nikons.

Purple Mountain Press is a publishing company committed to producing the best books of regional interest as well as bringing back into print significant older works. For a free catalog of more than 300 hard-to-find books about New York State, write Purple Mountain Press, Ltd., P.O. Box E3, Fleischmanns, New York 12430-0378, or call 914-254-4062, or fax 914-254-4476, or email Purple@catskill.net.

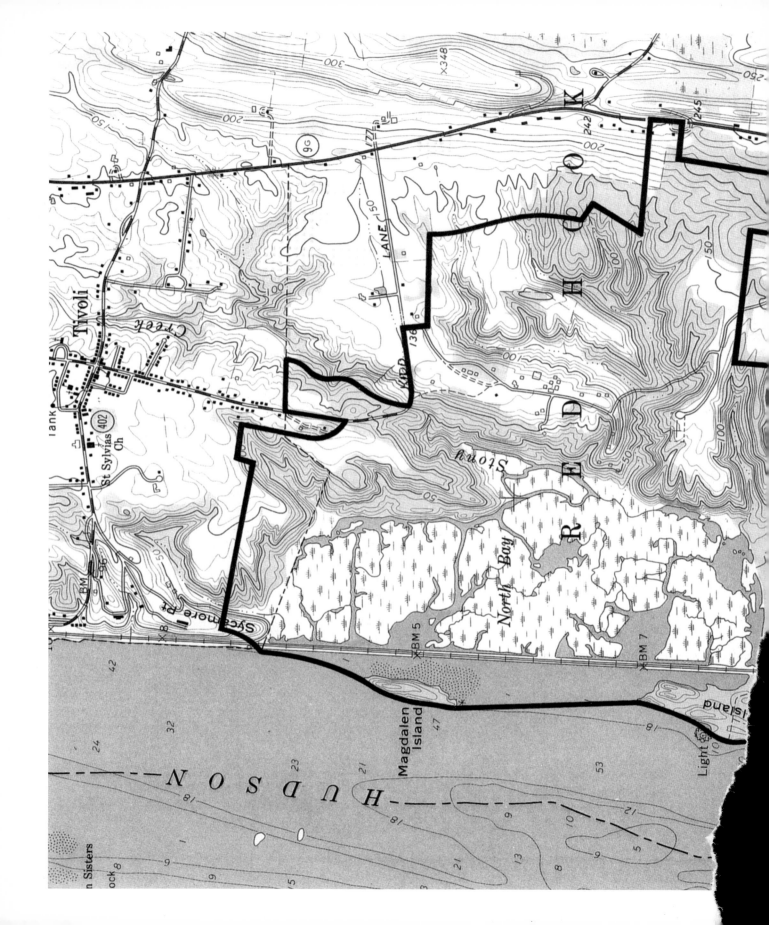